Ice Cream Poems

Ice Cream Poems
reflections on life with ice cream

Edited by Patricia Fargnoli

World Enough
Writers

Poetry
ISBN 978-1-937797-04-1

Cover photo by Lorraine Healy

Book Text and Cover Design by Tonya Namura
using Cherry Swash (display) and Gentium Basic (text)

World Enough Writers
PO Box 445
Tillamook. OR 97141

http://WorldEnoughWriters.com

WorldEnoughWriters@gmail.com

Forget art. Put your trust in ice cream.
　—Charles Baxter

　　Ice cream is exquisite. What a pity it isn't illegal.
　　—Voltaire

　　　I guess ice cream is one of those things that
　　　are beyond imagination.
　　　—L.M. Montgomery

TABLE OF CONTENTS

Ice Cream Poems

I Cold & Sweet Inside Us

Ice cream is happiness condensed.
—Jessi Lane Adams

*And is there any better way to prove your
burning love to a girl
than to give her ice-cream?*
—Richard D. Ware

*She could not have gazed at him with a
more rapturous intensity
if she had been a small child and he a
saucer of ice cream.*
—P. G. Wodehouse

Michael Dylan Welch

we walk the boardwalk hand in hand
    sharing ice cream
headaches

Margaret Hasse

SNOW ICE CREAM

Outside, white moths of flakes fill the air.

It's time to harvest snow.

The children and I feel sharp needles
in our bare hands that scoop snow
from the cleanest waves of white.

In the fields, snow blows through the lathes of snow
fences,
drifts onto the road like long thoughts escaping.

Her feet were cold when she lay for three days at home,
dying in a December long ago.

Back in the warm kitchen, it's her recipe we make:
whip an egg with cream and sugar.
Add the grit of nutmeg.
Pour onto the snowdrift in a blue bowl.
Stir. Stir.

We eat what we made,
taking the cold and the sweet inside us.

Wendy Elizabeth Ingersoll

SIXTY-EIGHTH BIRTHDAY

The steel band lady taps her sticks
across the globe, shimmers
gold bracelets down her arms, orange
skirt swirling round her hips—

my grandson toddles
close, shakes his hands and elbows,
everything he's got. We're in line
at Ben and Jerry's, waiting for
our special treat, her skirt echoes

the bugles of the trumpet vine
trimming our arbor, where children and grandchildren
flocked to watch me unwrap presents: books, cd's,

all their love I hoped. I'm approaching
the edge of my page, sometimes
I can't quite catch
the color of Middle C, is age 68
even on the spectrum. Orange sherbet,

I tell the girl at the window. Those trumpet bugles
shimmered in breeze as I opened gifts,
like a kind of vibrato. Like an echo

of birds serenading the day,
declaring territory, bragging about
feather-colors, trying
to attract the jennys, carry on
the species. If only

I could be so fearless, unambiguous,
if I could fill my outlook with orange trumpets,
sing out loud, everything I've got.

Judith Sanders

THE TREAT

At the ice cream counter the ample waitress
keeps scooping samples I don't want.
First a flavor called *White House*,
"created by Granddad after a trip to DC
at cherry blossom time." No self-respecting
tree ever produced fruits like these
red plastic chews, studding cold cotton balls
soaked in cough syrup. She chatters
about guys who stagger in for a beer,
about her favorite *phosphate*: "Hershey's,
seltzer, scoops of vanilla." I can feel myself
getting fat. She offers yet another spoon:
an Alpine peak of *Blueberry Creme*. It tastes
like shaving lather. But she's friendly;
it's a Tuesday afternoon; a few stools over,
a white-haired couple admire their twin
dripping sundaes. She strews rainbow
jimmies for a prancing toddler, even
adorns the dish with a shimmery ribbon.
The bell over the door jingles; in strut
stubbled guys in overalls, catcalling
for triple dips of *White House*.
                                    Sheltered
by my shoulder, my slender son solemnly
celebrates turning thirteen-and-a-half
with what to him is the tallest, creamiest
of chocolate milkshakes, the kind the angels
must sip in heaven. One taste and I feel
like rushing to the dentist, but my son
can handle sweetness. Happy half-birthday,

son. You're halfway between so many
things. I count out bills, stack emptied
spoons. Soon you'll suck up the last drops
and leave, the bell jingling behind you

Mary Ellen Talley

SESTINA FOR ICE CREAM

Dinner done at Shilshole Beach, we stand
at the counter for Little Coney's chocolate vanilla
    swirl cone.
Signature of summer, we lick a tongue-tip circle—
cold cold and cold again but smooth ice cream
before crunch of the wafer shell. We swallow
while sunset peaks to bend dusk into dark.

Sunset each evening bends dusk into dark
and even if we're walking elsewhere, we will stand
in line looking at the dairy case, swallow
one of 31 hand-scooped flavors into each cone,
elevating tongue-tip licks catching ice cream,
wrist twirl, lick in a circle.

Twirl of the wrist, lick in a circle
where vanilla is the antonym to every dark
licorice, rocky road, blackberry, cookie dough ice cream
but it is not necessary for everyone to stand
at a glassed-in dairy counter for the next cone
if the machine on the deck readies for our swallow.

Taste buds prepped ready for our swallow
after everyone gets a turn to crank many a full circle—
fatigue, salt and ice in the metal canister needn't land
    in a cone,
just another gallon of vanilla spooned upon dark
blueberry cobbler still warm in a 9"x 13" pan. Stand
lined up in the kitchen to scoop homemade ice cream.

Birthday party ready, scoop peppermint ice cream,
cut the cake. We'll sing to pecan praline, swallow
bubble gum, pistachio, rainbow sherbet. Next day stand
in line for a root beer float at the drive-in circle,
or dad brought home a jug of A&W and vanilla on a dark
evening to spoon into chilled mugs, so who needs a cone.

Spoon this evening, we don't need a cone.
It may be orange and white in a Dixie Cup ice cream
hiding in the freezer when I go downstairs in the
        cool dark
basement coming up with the flat wooden spoon. I'll
        swallow
cold flavors melting as my tongue moves in a circle.
Summer ends and vanilla is hands down favorite where
        we stand.

I stand on the beach holding the cone—
my tongue swirling, twirling circles of ice cream
as I swallow memory in the easy dark.

John Manesis

CITY PARK SUNDRIES
for Nick Manesis

In a 50s style cafe,
while sipping coffee,
I hear a fork ping,
a malt machine is whirring—
my father's face appears
in the mirror behind the soda fountain,
his thinning hair combed back,
that dimpled chin and prominent nose,
the serious look—

"All right, let's get to work,"
he decreed in a less complicated age
of one man, one vote rule.
With sleeves rolled up,
a tie tucked into his shirt,
he handed aprons to my brother and me
when we reported for duty at that store
in Denver he had bought the week before.
We would have rather been playing baseball
but in our fifteenth summer began
to sweep the floors, stock the shelves
and squeegee the windows clean,
learned to make correct change
and mastered the cash register,
became veteran soda jerks,
concocting sundaes, malts, and shakes,
without, as our father put it,
"giving away the store."
"Yes, ma'am," and "No, sir,"

were etched in our lexicon
as we sold a medley of goods—
bottles of Kaopectate, Geritol,
Anacin and Pepto-Bismol,
packs of Pall Malls, Old Golds
and Luckies that went for 25¢,
Mail Pouch and Red Man tobacco
old timers wadded into chaws,
Ex-lax or Feenamint for customers
who insisted on being "regular,"
the Alka Seltzer discs that fizzed
away in bubbly glasses.
For men and boys who would be men

and wanted "rubbers" or "prophylactics,"
we discreetly dispensed Trojans or Ramses.
And to the glee of eighteen year olds,
they could buy 3.2 beer to go,
including Sundays, as we hustled
to keep the coolers jammed with brands
like Coors and Falstaff, Tivoli and Hamms.

The footsteps of those who shared
that journey resonate in the halls
and corridors of memory—
the burly policeman, Leonard Johnson,
whose car rammed a tree on his last patrol,
an aging former boxer, Dempsey,
who heard the clang of phantom bells
as he lurched down the street,
Lee Hazelwood, the Cicero
of 21st and York, a cab driver
and ex-army officer whose dispatcher
is probably still trying to locate him,

Bobby Phelan with the auburn hair
and meteoric Irish temper,
the gentle Greek immigrant, old Angelo,
an employee whose candle burned down
on the cancer ward of the VA Hospital,
a wrinkled black man, George, who loved
King Edward cigars and charged them
until his monthly check arrived,
then always paid his bill to "Mr. Nick."

"Do you want a refill?...
Sir, would you like a refill?"
the teenage waitress asks.
I catch a final glimpse of him,
lay a hand over the cup
and say, "I wish I could."

Michael Brockley

ODE TO BLUE MOON ICE CREAM

In a Muncie Baskin-Robbins, you sampled Blue Moon
ice cream while Linda teased a double chocolate fudge
with her tongue. It was the summer of shining stars
and earth, wind and fire. It was the year of the man
who would be king. You crooned *Blue Moon* to her after
ordering your cone. *Without a dream in my heart.* But
you nibbled at the blue dessert with the caution you
brought to swallowing strawberry licorice for love.
Blue Moon. Linda dancing to *Jet* and *Bluebird*. The taste
of crooning doo wop to the moon of the thirteenth
month. She left you for a man who drove a red Firebird.
Left you with a song without a chorus.

Until the year high school girls in pink t-shirts and
cut-off jeans sold scoops of Blue Moon in a mom-
and-pop shop you discovered at the crossroads
between Middletown, USA and the rural mailboxes of
Cammack. A round carton tucked in the freezer behind
Butter Pecan. Beside Mint Chocolate Chip. Route 66
license plates tilted on the wall behind the register.
Lithographs of Cadillac Ranch centered between the
storefront picture windows. Above your booth, 45s
by Vampire Weekend and the Kings of Leon haloed
a TouchTunes jukebox. Where you discovered the
Marcels' ballad on the afternoon when your blue moon,
at last, had turned to gold.

Michael Estabrook

FORGIVING US STILL

We're in P-town sightseeing when a bunch
of motorcyclists ride up on their smoking hogs.
I stop window-shopping
to have a look, the butter crunch ice cream
dripping down the sugar cone into
the palm of my hand.

They're older with cigarettes smoldering
in dark-bearded faces, long gray hair
protruding beer bellies
bluish-gray tattoos.

They have hard-looking women with them
in shiny hip boots, tangled blonde hair
peace sign earrings and love beads too
like in the 60s.

But nobody's worried as they park
their bikes with a clatter and dismount
because the lettering on their jackets reads:
VIETNAM VETS

And somehow we feel safe then certain
and solemn because they're bigger than life
for they've been to hell and returned
to tell us about it and live among us forgiving us still.

Rebe Huntman

MOTHER WITH PAUL NEWMAN AND SMALL AXIS

If I could see nothing but the quiver
on her red lips, I would know everything
about the girl she clasped inside her handbag.
I would know this was a café where doors spun open
before they closed and a woman might
for a moment remember who she was.
If I could see nothing but her eyes I would know
how my father warned her not
to embarrass herself, and I could reconstruct
the night my mother met Paul Newman—
How, one hand holding a vanilla cone,
she smoothed her skirt with the other
and went to him, this her only offering—
She was a fan. How she grasped for the next
slice where the circles of their lives
might intersect—the weather, his latest film,
two smiles flashing before exhausting themselves
and my mother re-joins my father, still bursting
with the largeness of the world.
I could fill her vast purse with dreams
of inhabiting the center of someone's universe
the way stars do. I could slip her girlhood in my pocket
and, wearing my questions like
tiny Rorschachs webbing at the corners of my own lip,
I could become the woman who turns,
brilliant, as Paul Newman calls her back,
every nerve in the place tuned to hers as he tells her
Ma'am. Tells her, Ma'am.
Tells her—Ma'am, I think you dropped your

ice cream in your purse.
If I could trace the fall
of her shoulders, the stain caught between
her hands, I would know what tied
her to the small axis of our lives.

Barbara Crooker

SUGAR

My mother is a hungry ghost. She comes to me in dreams,
asking, where's the applesauce? The kind *you* make?
Cooked with the skins on, whirled with cinnamon
and nutmeg, swirled through a food mill, smooth fruit
separated from skins, cores, seeds. Shouldn't this
    sweetness
exist in the afterlife? Yet I've heard that's what angels
    crave
those times they're glimpsed, partly visible, a rustle of
    wings,
an opening in the air. Apparently, they shimmer,
made of gossamer and light. We always long
for what we don't have, and they yearn to be incarnate,
to know the hunger of the tongue. Filaments of cotton
    candy,
fistfuls of sugar, the long slow drip of honey and molasses.
I tried to sweeten my mother's last days, bringing
her a deconstructed sundae—coffee ice cream in one cup,
hot fudge in another, whipped cream in a third. But her
    hunger
is not appeased. She still longs for this world, its
    confectionary
splendor. She would, if she could, open her mouth
like a bird or a baby, and let me spoon it in.

Fran Markover

BITTERSWEET

The night of the burial, we head for ice cream.
At Purity, my husband recalls his father's love—
baseball—a storyboard of bunts, comebacks,
blowouts. After games, we'd toast each nail-biter
with malteds whenever Finger Lakes Seniors
won big. His dad, as if hearing cries of *good eye*,
would size up each Rocky Road or Mud Pie.

Thinking of his father, my husband orders
double peppermint chip. Notes how Dixie Cups
are smaller than when his folks were alive.
Can't anything stay the same? Will Monster Cones
shrink to Kiddie scoops?

We taste the bittersweet, sure that my father-
in-law would've ranted at chocolate morsels
so puny they slip unnoticed, shrouded inside
all the confection. We sit in the car, bundled
in parkas, fine-tune *Bound for Glory* on the radio.
Eat Dessert First blinks, reddens the wall.
In January chill, our breath forms a milky way.

ICE CREAM WITH WHIPPED CREAM FOR OUR FIFTIETH

*What lies behind us and what lies before us
are small compared to what lies within us.*
   —Ralph Waldo Emerson

All eight of us savor *Eis mit Schlagsahne*
in Leonberg's town square, where we've come
to show children and grandchildren
my father's birthplace, # 18 *Marktplatz*, the half-
timbered house dating from 1711, where his father
had his tinsmith's shop on the ground floor,
later dying in wartime.

"Johannes Keppler lived across the way in the 1500s,"
father would say. A plaque confirms it.
This an inward journey as I stare
at my son's jaw line, so like his brother's,
a son lost a quarter century ago.
Love, a joy we borrow.
The church bell tolls another hour.

Earlier by our hotel we filmed my grandmother's
house, rural once, now city—a store, EURO BAZAR
at street level. She, my most faraway relative,
closest to me. A story-teller, a star I orbited
on her visits to us—when she discovered Manhattans—
on return flights, even in her eighties
holding up a card printed: MANHATTAN, BITTE
when the stewardess asked, *Kaffee, Tee, oder Milch?*—
later writing she was moved to the last empty row

where she could sing her hymns and yodel.
My fingernails and feet are like hers.

I came to see her when I was twenty, snapped
a last black and white photo of her waving goodbye
from her upstairs window—a fly zigzagging in
to her *Apfel Kuchen*, to rest perhaps on the pillow
she embroidered: *Nur eine Viertelstunde*—
only a quarter hour—her nap time,
when her head dropped to her neckline lace,
the oval garnet brooch she left me:
gold filigree, trumpet clasp.
I waved back, *Auf Wiedersehen*,
until we meet again, before turning to leave.

Karen Skolfield

DURIAN PROHIBITED IN THIS HOTEL

So says the sign by the elevators, first in Malay, then English. Durian: a fruit with a smell "considered offensive by some." Now we're curious, want to be the best American tourists ever. Already we've used the squat toilets without complaint. What can't we do if we put our minds to it? In our pockets the currency of colorful ringgits has something to say. At the durian ice cream stand the worker hears our accent, assures us we'll soon be fans. We want to be fans. We're patting ourselves on the back, inventing stories: *yeah, the smell but best ice cream ever, most tourists don't like it, wish we could get it in the States,* etc. On the counter are football-sized durians, bristled. My son can't resist touching spiky things. "Hard, but not pokey," he declares. Flinted Rs, the New England brass in our voices. There's a smell but we wave away doubts, accept our cones. The worker beams, watches our faces as we take licks. We say: "Oh, wow, thank you! We're going to enjoy our ice cream outside." He touches his right palm to the center of his chest, both a farewell and gesture of thanks. In our hands, shame in the shape of a cone; in our mouths, the cringe of American palates. "Don't spit it out," I hiss at the kids. Still eating: "I am not letting this thing beat me," my son says, but quietly, in case Malaysia is listening.

Shahé Mankerian

DEFINING DIVORCE AT FIVE

My daughter says, "God designed the autistic
brain with purple sails. They take daily voyages

without clear vision. They're smart,
but their temper melts like ice cream sundae.

They feel congested when too many people
crowd around them. See that crow?

Even though it's black, they see the rainbow
flapping in a cage. They're weird.

Like Chantal's dad; he's wired differently.
He left them because he doesn't want to live

with them anymore. Chantal said her daddy
saw everything as caged, crowded,

full of pecking crows. So his ice cream
has melted like a black lava. He's autistic."

Janet Bowdan

HOLY COW

I'm trying to list
the redeeming features of this
Little League game,
now in its 4th inning, 3rd hour,
my kid's team 7 runs behind—
it's not freezing,
in fact, Blair's promised
to pay for ice cream for the whole team
if they get a double play;
the view of the Mt. Holyoke range
across the fields is lovely;
small planes are buzzing happily
in the blue sky—
when we're electrified by a pop foul
that plummets into the dug-out
onto the head
of Luke, the ball-magnet
who would prefer to be home
quietly reading *Calvin & Hobbes*.
It's the second time he's been hit
this game, upping his average
to 1.3 giant bruises per game.
And he doesn't even get a walk
for this one! I do have a lollipop
on hand, and fortunately
he thinks sugar is an excellent substitute
for athletic success. Moreover,
somehow this has changed our luck:
Cal and TJ, Lexie & Noah, Heath
and Maggie all get hits or walks, steal,

get runs. Cody makes fabulous catches
at third and almost a double play with Cal.
We don't win, but hey,
it's not about winning: it's about
the ice cream at the end of the game.
Cody gets black raspberry with
colored sprinkles; Cal gets a root beer
float; Luke goes home to read.

Laura Foley

THE HAPPY APARTMENT

Seven floors above Broadway,
above the ice cream shop,
seven flights of stairs
I descend pregnant, each evening
for my fresh-dipped
coffee-almond ice cream bar,
then climb back home.
Seven for exercise,
for the lucky number.
Seven stories soaring over the avenue.
More than seven large windows
over a leafy green campus,
St. John the Divine
gold in the morning light.
Three of us in two narrow rooms,
my desk in the corridor,
books towered everywhere,
our young dog's nursery
a closet in the hall,
where she gives birth to six
beautiful long-haired mutts;
and I in the bed,
a second blond boy.

Elissa Hoffman

STEVE'S ICE CREAM IS GONE

it was the early 70s
war & just beyond, love
a hate war & a love war
a freakin' unnatural rootless time, sad
daft time draft time & us smoke-brained
craving a way out a way in &
me all natural frizzed out &
braless denimed up & running down
it was a break my heart & keep on truckin' time
a cruel time Jimi & Janis
just gone & waves more in Nam
well all times are cruel, but at least
Dylan Zeppelin The Byrds Stones Who &
Moody Blues spread their
sound wave haze
clear & hazy both together—
but most of all for me
it was *Steve's Ice Cream*

& fuck I'm pushing 70s now
& you know sometimes I stare out &
can't tell if it's snowing
think I see stuff flying out there
but maybe it's just fog or dust or dirt
or old snow thrown off the roof by the wind
or just my imagination
but *Steve's Ice Cream!!* yeah

I felt fine & wild then &
went to Steve's each day &

even so a tailor years later said
she'd never seen a lady's belly *so* flat!—
no more, & now the sky is hazy
hazier & hazier—
it used to be more blue
now more cities are burnt to hell
Steve's Ice Cream is Gone
cars ditched & stripped
& people dead
but *Steve's...*&

I'd wait in that crazy long line
that Somerville folks knew so well &
we'd snake down the pavement
kissing the blue sky 'cause
Steve's had mix-in's
the first! &
rolled the ice cream out
on a big marble slab all white & sparkly
& stuffed it full—M&M's berries pretzels nuts—
& then I sat down with that cone
at the old wooden tables & chairs
all painted so pale a purple
a lavender maybe but bright &
collected by Steve who knows where &
I ate my heart out!

but now I found out last night
that *Steve's* is gone—went & closed 2009
& moved...I forget where
& now it's called—Herrell's!
Herrell's
hell

my heart's scooped out

'cause Steve,
that place, that place,
it was something I needed,
held onto
not just then either

cold ice cream melts
& time is slick
milk & ice
a marble slab
no holding on
no going back

Aimee Harris

THE WAR WAS WON WITH ICE CREAM

He was off limits, an American soldier in France.
You tell me my grandfather tempted you
with a block of tea on a chilly winter day,
but what really thawed your heart was ice cream.

He'd visit your father's photo shop
in the depths of the Paris Metro,
purchasing more film in his limited French
than any one person could ever shoot.

One day he brought in an ad for ice cream
served on base. It had been a war
of Brussels sprouts and charred meats;
this must have seemed a mirage.

There you ate two sundaes,
one strawberry
and one pineapple
along with a chocolate milkshake

and later forced down
dinner at home
the dutiful daughter filled
with a secret hunger now.

One day you were walking through a park
covered in snow the color of vanilla ice cream.
A branch sent a chilly mass down on the two of you
as if a sign to hurry him on his way,

he asked you to marry him in English
and you answered in the same, a language
that would become your own
even though certain letters such as h's still escape you.

And so I knew how to spot true love,
it is one beyond language
that melts in your heart
like the sweetest delicacy.

Four notes found in the utensil drawer of my dad's assisted living kitchenette a few days before he died:

There is some
ice cream in
the ice cream in
the refrigerator.
Please help yourself.
Please yourself.

*

There is some ice
cream in the. Please
help yourself with
the provided with the
provided spoon.

*

Please use the spoon
to enjoy to ice.

*

There is some ice
cream.

Jeanne Ferran

HELEN

Dust settled on the costume jewelry
in the display case she stood behind.
Coifed in monochromatic jewel tones,
statuesque, in scuffed heels,
she observed her empire,
her catlike eyes veiled by false blue lenses.

She had been told all her life that she was beautiful—
a badge she proudly wore since childhood.
Her love waxed and waned
with my mother's weight and hair color
and number of suitors.

Yet Helen's eyes were only for my grandfather—
busily making po-boy sandwiches for
the business lunch crowd:
men who flung their ties over their shoulders
as roast beef gravy dripped down French bread
and pooled onto butcher paper lined with onion rings
A Barq's pinning down the upturned corner.
Food and drink she rang up at the counter for 50 years
but never touched.

Years later, she lies in a nursing home,
her porcelain skin free from makeup,
her eyes, green as moss.
She is a child again.
She spends her days looking for reason
on the ceiling, humming melodies
of long-forgotten Big Band songs.

The remnants of her life—
an afghan blanket,
old photographs, a plastic flower,
Mardi Gras doubloons,
a silver-plated mirror, a box of rings
that no longer fit over the knots of her knuckles—
surround her.
Her body, freed by the Alzheimer's
that prevented her
from counting calories,
purging dinners,
no longer denies the pleasure
of her own family's livelihood.
Her paper skin wraps around her body—
full for the first time.

I sit with the shadow of the woman I knew,
scooping ice cream on a metal spoon.
I wipe the melted chocolate
from the corners of her pallid lips.
"More," she mutters,
when I show her the empty bowl.

Esther Altshul Helfgott

I DREAM OF UNCLE BENNY AND STRAWBERRIES

I'm eight years old, and Uncle Benny doesn't have to go back to the Rosewood State Training Center for Boys out in Reisterstown, Maryland any more. He never ever has to go back because he lives in our house now and guess what his room is filled with strawberry ice cream. The walls are covered with ice cream. The chairs are. Uncle Benny's bed is made of strawberry, and the carpet is strawberry plush. In my dream, Uncle Benny's sitting at his desk, which Mother and I bought for him. The desk is the color of strawberry. Uncle Benny's sitting at the desk and he's writing. He's copying letters out of my first-grade reader, my Dick and Jane book. All of a sudden, a strawberry walks into his room. She touches Uncle Benny's shoulder. She touches his shoulder and it's no longer twisted into his sternum. Now, the strawberry touches Uncle Benny's spine, and when she touches his knees, he gets out of his chair, stands straight to the sky and throws his cane into the strawberry waste basket. He bends down to pick up his cane and it turns into a strawberry ice cream soda. Uncle Benny drinks the ice cream soda and in a voice that is no longer unintelligible, he reads Dick and Jane to me, the whole story, about Sally and Spot and the little kitty, Puff. I awaken from my dream and run into the kitchen to find Mother wiping strawberry ice cream off of Uncle Benny's unshaven chin, which won't get shaved until Uncle Izzy comes home from the print shop. Then we'll get in the car and drive out to Rosewood where we'll leave my Uncle Benny on the steps of his cottage.

II This Sweet, Sweet World

Have you ever spent days and days and days making up flavors of ice cream that no one's ever eaten before? Like chicken and telephone ice cream? Green mouse ice cream was the worst.
I didn't like that at all.
—Neil Gaiman

I had a dream about you. I licked your cone of ice cream. It was envelope flavored.
—Melody Sohayegh

From the outside, my life may look chaotic, but inside I feel like some kind of monk licking an ice cream cone while straddling a runaway horse.
—Tom Robbins

Barbara Crooker

L'ATELIER ROSE, 1911, HENRI MATISSE

I came back to Paris free of the Louvre's influence and
heading for color.
—Henri Matisse

It's like being back in the womb, isn't it, these walls of pink,
this floor one rose shade deeper? I think about my middle
daughter, five months pregnant. Her baby's grown
from an orange seed to a green olive to a plum. Now
it's the size of a boneless chicken breast. What is it
about babies that makes us think of food? And what
is it about this color that makes us think of health?
Because we say *in the pink* when we're feeling fine?
Because roses blush in different shades? Because some
kir drizzled in Champagne makes it *royale*? But

if you get a pink slip, you've been canned, and watch
out for those elephants on parade. No one aspires
to a pink-collar job. And no girl wants a bunch
of carnations, smelling of cloves and maiden aunts.
The sunset pinkens the sky in the west, and I'm
tickled pink, thinking of you. Matisse's studio glows,
suffused in light, the inside of a satin slipper. Pink
the edges of my heart, cut them into scallops, make
them whirly. Imagine strawberry ice cream, rhubarb
compote, candy hearts. This sweet, sweet world.

BAKED RED MULLET

Giverny's in France, of course— the bus left Paris
early and off we went, which has been scrawled on
dozens of postcards and immortalized in photos (not to
mention poems.) Meanwhile the fish in my kitchen is
from Florida waters, fresh off the docks—but my mind's
quirky, gone back to France. I look for inspiration or for
luck into the gift shop cookbook. . . under Mullet.

It's full of gossip: Claude Monet was a rascal. What he
did with Alice was the death of his wife Camille (it says
here) but they moved to Giverny from Vetheuil on barges.
Amid recipes comments, austerely: Hordes of sightseers
cannot quite obliterate the artist's way of life—vistas of
green swamp to be glimpsed from his bedroom windows,
water-lilies to paint and the fresh fish.

The recipe calls for 4 red mullet, with or without
livers—to your taste. Ubiquitous garlic and onion join
chopped black olives with basil leaves torn, bruised and
braised in oil. (was it Alice B.Toklas who wrote there's
no good cooking that doesn't involve pain?) Or no good
mullet should die in vain.

Down at the bottom there's more gossip. Julie Manet
(Berthe Morisot's daughter) is described as "fazed" by
Claude's table manners— soup all over that great beard—
ending quite appropriately with a hint of dessert— she
loved his paintings: especially the series of Rouen
Cathedrals which remind her of pink skies of morning,
seen as "dollops of strawberry ice-cream."

Chella Courington

MAMA'S ORCHID
after a painting by Georgia O'Keeffe

girl, just look at that flower

all green and yellow
swimming together
spilling
over the edge
like rainbow ice cream
mama made in july
and spooned into glass cups
that slipped
from our sticky hands
crashing
on the black and white
linoleum she laid
when too old
to bear children.

just look at those petals

fringed in lavender
a feather boa
she tossed
over her shoulder
cascading
down a satin back
saturday nights
as daddy dipped her
to radio blues
with us praying

for long legs
and to stay up past nine
when ella and billie
brought it on home.

never cared for real orchids

those hothouse types
too busy
being fussed over
still don't bloom
like that purple flower
mama loved
to wear on her birthday
and afterward
stored it in the icebox
till petals turned brown.

Julia Park Tracey

CARDAMOM

In Boonville, they've a language of their own:
a word for a hussy (*madge*) and a word for girlfriend
    (*applehead*)
a word for a tall tale (*Johnem*) and a word for a
    hangover (*jimheady*).
Boontling, they call it—
a twin-language. It's gibberish to outsiders,
to the Sassenach who cross borders,
enter the realm that sleeps
in fog and forest.
Around the winding back roads of scrub and rock and
    creek—
through timbertrails used to pillage the redwoods for
    beam and mast;
now vineyards, hilly rows of magical vines—
and sheep
And goats and a shaggy thing that looks like a yak—
we break into sunshine and beer gardens,
a bar called The Buckhorn
with a chandelier made from deer antlers.
For the price of a soda,
we can use the can, eyeball the regulars,
then escape to the dusty sidewalk again,
and the rest of our journey.
The scent of coffee arrests me.
We pass through swinging doors into a former Old West
barbershop or shoeshine, its origins indeterminate;
suitable antiques dot the walls.
No *madges* would have been served,
but I ask for a tiny taste on a tinny spoon,

and take my hussy cone of sweetcool cardamom
    ice cream
That tastes of India and the great Ganges,
of bindi dots and silken saris,
the bright curry colors of a culture 10,000 miles from this
cloaked village, this
solipsism in a redwood grove.
I taste the foreign as a foreigner in a
strange and willful place,
and we drive onward,
spices lingering on my tongue.

Michael Meyerhofer

ICE CREAM

Ancient Persians made poetry
by pouring grape juice over snow.
Later, they used rose water,
ice mixed with saffron.
The Arabs were the first to add
milk and sugar, though
the Chinese used saltpeter
to chill their poems into sorbet.

Nowadays, poetry can be served
in little dishes with sprinkles
at parties and buffets,
savored by the rich and poor alike,
though the best method
remains to pour your poetry
in a waffle cone and let it bleed
its words all over your lap.

If someone notices, feign
embarrassment and tell them
you have to go home and change,
but really, wear that stain
for as long and as proudly as you can.
It is a boon. It is a blessing.
And every passing snicker—a sign
that you are half an emperor.

ODE TO LAVENDER ICE CREAM
*with appreciation to Elevated Ice Cream Candy Shop,
Port Townsend, WA*

Because the naked spoon
scalds your palette without it.

Holy trinity, it is the field,
and the animal of the field,
stirred with the root of the earth.

Ice cream will resist your muscle,
resist being scooped up with its soft tension,
semi-solid withholding.
Yet it will give itself wholly to you
at first contact with your erotic breath.

Like the sea, you are both born of salt.

This confection is obviously tenuous
even under the best conditions,
which you do not like to admit is true
of your mortal self.

Because lavender knows the wind's secrets
and keeps them.

Because ice cream knows what happens
when the door thuds closed
and is not tainted by that bitter, darkful dark.

Its sweetness, from generations of plantation bondage,
tunnels freedom
through your organs.

Forgiveness is never so easy as after
you have encountered lavender ice cream,
surrendered all your resentments.

The sight of it in a white bowl will remind you
of the first snowman you built in childhood,
or of the white kitten
your uncle saved from the burning barn.

If you listen intently, you will hear
lavender ice cream's song,
not like an angel's
which is fraught with blood,
but like a coqui's call the initial hour of spring
in a country you will never visit,
or like a xylophone tinkling softly in the place
where your lover rests,
dreaming only of the blameless skin
on the back of your neck.

Marilyn L. Taylor

REVERIE IN SAPPHICS, WITH FRIES

Straight-spined girl—yes, you of the glinting earrings,
amber skin and sinuous hair: what happened?
you've no business lunching with sticky children
here at McDonald's.

Are they yours? How old were you when you had them?
You are far too dazzling to be their mother,
though I hear them spluttering *Mommy Mommy*
over the Muzak.

Do you plan to squander your precious twenties
wiping ice cream dripping from little fingers,
drowning your ennui in a Dr. Pepper
from the dispenser?

Were I you for one schizophrenic moment,
I'd display my pulchritude with a graceful
yet dismissive wave to the gathered burghers
feeding their faces—

find myself a job as a super-model,
get me to those Peloponnesian beaches
where I'd preen all day with a jug of ouzo
in my bikini.

Would I miss the gummy suburban vinyl,
hanker for the Happiest Meal on Main Street?
Or would one spectacular shrug suffice for
begging the question?

Sandra Anfang

POSTCARD POEM

Dear Caleb,

Here on Kauai they speak English and Japanese
but on the radio it's hula 24/7.
The land is lush—the color of a child's broccoli tree.
Red dirt gets in our eyes and nostrils.
We visited Hanalei Bay. I swear I saw
Puff the Magic Dragon lift his scaly head
above the green waves.
Every day at three we find ourselves
at the shave ice shop in Kapaa
which is curious, since we both forgot our watches.
We always order a scoop of vanilla ice cream under the ice.
We've sampled every beach;
the public one boasts the brightest parrotfish.
Clay bought himself a native flute;
the carver gave him a free lesson on the fly.
We may not be coming home anytime soon.

Aloha,
Sasha

Deborah H. Doolittle

THE ROCKY ROAD TO DUBLIN

is not a flavor of ice cream.
It is not a road. There can be
no rocks, pebbles or otherwise,
strewn about it. The way we were
taught to sing made us seem like larks
in the morning, scattered across
the meadow, rising in the sky
to greet the sun. We were drunk
on the words, stumbling into
the chorus. Each and every
time counting ourselves lucky
and Irish enough to know
to end it where we had begun.

Lucia Cherciu

ICE CREAM SWIRLS
Romania, 1984

At noon we headed across town
 to the milk factory.
We were twelve and five. The more
 we walked, the farther
we got, spinning in circles,
 tracing our steps backwards.
We crossed a construction site
 only to find the exit was closed
and we had to turn and stare
 at the delicate forklift crane,
wonder how it stood in the air.
 Roads spun and spiraled,
imaginary ice cream swirled,
 and after three hours of walking
we sat on a bench in a park
 swearing that this was the way.
Streets were all straight, leading
 to some statue, a palace,
the Party headquarters, and yet that day
 the road crumbled, sent us back
where we started. Ice cream curls
 filled the afternoon, illusory
flavors of vanilla, chocolate,
 and strawberry, the whole town
turned into an ice cream cone,
 savory whirls, cool taste,
while the sun melted the pavement
 until our shoes sank in the sidewalk,
dust accumulating in mounds
 where stray dogs bathed,
shook their fur, thirsty and starved.

Erin Redfern

FINALE IN MARIANNE'S MANDARIN CHOCOLATE

1. Satsuma

Lonely self-pollinator, your white blossoms
give themselves to no one: you of all citrus
know the sweetness of being one's own.
When winter threatens, your leathery purse grows
big with its small fortune. Virgin fruit, hesperidium,
perhaps you are missing your entourage, those nymphs
who guarded your gold at the far shores of the world.
You traded them for the sensation you made
when you came to America, arriving across frozen plains
in whole box cars painted orange. Treasured globe,
you fill the toes of Christmas stockings and spill
across New Year's tabletops. We keep you
in circulation, a juicy gesture meaning
for you all things abundant and good.

2. Cacao

Chocolate is a machete hacking the blushing, fulsome
      fruit,
fingers prying ripe kernels from their inner cob. It is
      work,
the beans broken, the nibs roasted and ground, refined,
conched, smoothed, kneaded, tempered, heated, cooled.
It is transport and trade--baskets, carts, quays, ocean
      liners.
It is carriage wheels clattering down rain-streaked lanes,
a sealed letter requiring delivery posthaste and leading

to creased satin, bruised skin, a tropical heat stirred
with a long metal spoon, a shaken pan, a sonata on the
    tongue,
a song that sings only of its own longing to be sung.

3. Brahms

Emperor of Penny Candy,
which you handed out to children on your walks,
you were equally attentive to adults
and once begged the pardon
of anyone you had neglected to insult.
Wanting to heat your listeners from the inside,
like Chekov you vowed *to be more cold.*
So your strings keen through mountain passes,
invoke an avalanche of ivory keys,
scour the rock face clean. Loyal Sherpa,
you've hauled these notes to the snowy crest,
unpacked them at the feet of Himalayan gods.
Now rest. Watch the emulsion of sky
and clementine sun. With your icy mind
make hymns to strife; with the milk
of your talent, churn songs of delight.

Susan Rich

ELEVATED
On Barack and Michelle Obama's first date,
they went to see a movie and then out for ice cream.

Here is where the traveler
seeks to taste imagination,

load it on her tongue
and let it linger—

hours, even years, if that's
what the flavor calls for—

to stare behind each sliding
door of Amaretto, Ginger,

and Blind Love. To pray
among the parlor's pyramids

of fluted parfait cups,
the hot red vinyl booths.

Waffle cones sugar
the high season air

of a rainbowed show
where all that matters

in the end (and long before)
is the house-mix

scooping rhythm
of lavender in chocolate—

an orange-chocolate swirl
of blue sky world.

Shirley J. Brewer

KEEPER OF THE MOON

Monhegan Island, off the coast of Maine.
Orange and purple swirls
paint a sherbet sunset treat,
dessert at the end of day.

These colors conjure you, except
you'd pass up sherbet
for a double scoop of nonfat ice cream.
You slipped away so fast.

I take comfort in your new role
mixing night sky confections,
no one better to flavor the stars.
The moon could use a little more sugar.

The lighthouse blinks our secret code.
How I miss the way you held me.

Jill McCabe Johnson

NORTH BEACH, LOW TIDE

When for a minute or ten of our stretch of a walk
on beach and rocks spread like dark eggs
wet under barnacles and broken shells, when the sun
slipped beneath a point low
                              on the bent horizon
of Saturna and Pender Islands, and the below-
sides of clouds flushed in foggy shades the tint
of yellowed paper or the last calendula, bristled
by northerly winds,
                      we spotted a split pear
of basalt and granite, pink on one half,
near-black on the other, sky and horizon a smear
of ice cream and mud, and you said, *We're overdue
for the big one,*
                  a seismic event and tsunami,
nine-point-oh on the Richter, and the whelp
of a seal barked or was it a heron. *I love you,*
I said, and the seaweed smelled of tumbling and smelt.

BEACH CONCESSION STAND ON LONG ISLAND SOUND

All sluggish spring, I watched
the trucks import tawny sand
from somewhere else,
bulldozing Ransom Beach
and raking the season smooth.
Day by day, this took exactly forever.
Waiting for the light to lengthen,
I rearranged thirty-three flavors of summer,
read a single Chekhov novel,
memorizing the choppy names,
my tongue thick with Cyrillic,
closed my eyes to the widening waterfront
and envisioned a great bird's wings
shaping the white air.

Then, on still-grey, early afternoons,
stray bodies, brave or stupid,
began to skirt the slack water.
The sky grew hazy
and the smell of brine built in the air
until finally I woke
to a warm mesh of sunlight.

Everything that matters is surf.
As a child, I was evacuated
from Venice during the floods
in the gilded summer of 1966,
and, as that child, I loved
the fierce frenzy of water

until police pulled us away
under noon darkness.
Now, I depend on water's calm attraction
for livelihood on this strip of erosion and ocean.
Striped awning uncurled,
I place a lightning whelk shell in the showcase
as billows of bodies parade past
and kites quilt the sky, their wooden ribs
straining against the wind.
The open window-stall looks
across to Greenwich, Connecticut
where the gold on the buildings' windows ascends
and the light runs slippery off them.

Days expend in a swelter of profit,
the thrum of the refrigeration unit
in a cold sweat.
Soon, I begin to recognize
the familiars,
note how they daily nestle
on their same spot of sand.
I furrow hills of ice-cream
and keep a nervous eye on the sky-line,
the particular swells and shapes of cloud-breath,
holding to the ransom of weather.
Hearing the gurgles of foreign languages,
young, timbered voices screaming
and blending with seagull-caw,
I watch the white skins

dive into the breach, their bodies
a cataract in the Sound's cornea,
splintering the strange, amber glimmers
that seem to well from deep water.

Black-tipped terns smudge the sky
till, gradually, the season ebbs of light.
My mark is how the boardwalk
thins of bodies, how deeply light
has carved their suits on their skins.
The sun pivots in retrograde
and I am left to count the shimmery coins,
buy potato chips and graphic novels
to prop near the couch,
think of buying a new freezer, a fresh sign.
On the quieting land spit,
I walk the stretch of my rented domain,
retreat to a highland view home,
waiting out the chill and thaw
for the unencumbered, frilly waves,
the many flavors of summer,
the generations of water.

John Rowe

HAPPINESS

Who says happiness
can't sit and wait
at a bus stop
even if the bus
never arrives?
I see happiness
sitting there alone
scribbling down a poem.
Truth is
happiness is not alone.
A crow in a nearby tree
keeps one eye on happiness.
Happiness is old and wise
but doesn't feel that way.
Now I see happiness
turn into a child
with an ice cream cone.
Three scoops
of favorite flavors.
Before long
laughter shows up
and sits down
next to happiness.
A certain kind
of music follows
to last a lifetime.

Joaquín Zihuatanejo

WE GAVE ICE CREAM TO JESUS

He leaned into the wind
behind him
a mesquite tree
bowed to the storm
both at the point of breaking
but enduring—

The light quickly changed from yellow to red

It was raining
a pack of dogs ran by

    Do two dogs constitute a pack?

    No se, pero el amor es una perra

You said that,
Your voice full of poetry

    I want the gray to envelope me

More poetry

He was a *viejito*

    Una pobre alma perdida

the kind of man who resents the word Chicano
because it implies war
and we have not been warriors since the Aztecas ruled
he would argue

He asked us for an offering

We gave him three dollars
our umbrella
and a quart of Mexican vanilla ice cream

I had just purchased for the woman
who rolled the window down
to offer him the gifts

> *Gracias*
> *Bendiga a ti y a tú familia*
>
> *¿Como se llama?*

Not knowing why I asked

> *Me llamo Jesús,*

he said in a voice
deep and dark as well water

We rolled the window up
drove off
not looking back
and left him
somewhere behind us
in the gray

Molly Tenenbaum

I LIVE IN A YELLOW ICE CREAM TRUCK

Red script flourishes, circling itself.
A blue square, one per side, sets off a white swan.

It was the rubber gasket
compressing
that whispered the hither.

I wondered, at first,
was it all one space, or did each door close
on its own small box?

At the back, a pull-down gate.
A little bed, a book, a pair of socks.
The inside walls are quilted tin.

The swan, daubed gray for shadows,
jogs as the truck jogs, over a bump,

and who knows if that counts
as motion—not even the blue
she's painted moving through moves,
her angle depends on the truck, on where

it's going, and under it,
on streets ascending, and under them,
on the whole dark dirt world, a city itself,
of mica and sand, wire and pipe.

I don't believe one world is more real than another.

Remember when they sent people to caves
to see when they would sleep?

One little railing for earrings and a mirror,
and for the night, a wide-mouth jar.

It would be better, I admit, with windows.
At night, hatches latched, it's pitch till morning.

What do I miss? Air.
I love the blanket-stitched sides
and the rumble of warming.

Darling, why am I sad?
There's nothing like a cubby.

Nothing like a pair of boots
and a bed that folds up.

Jeanne Thomas

GREEN

Green...
the park where
officers ride horses
and an ice cream man
sells his sweets
to little kids who
run and tumble
in the Green
where I once
have been.

Michael Sweeney

IN THE MELONE DUSK

In Piazza San Marco,
in the afternoon heat,
a dark-skinned, elegant woman
in white dress and beige heels,
carries her clutch
across the empty stone.
She does not distinguish
the glistening sweat on her olive face
from the melone gelato
smeared across it.
As she walks past and tosses her hair,
the cone in her hand drips vibrant orange.
She loses herself
as her composure dissolves
into the afternoon heat,
in the melone dusk,
of Piazza San Marco.

Patrick Swaney

THE DAY WE NEVER MET

Perhaps there is nothing better than walking
a summer street eating an ice cream cone. Except

maybe walking a summer street eating an ice cream cone
as it starts to rain, and someone on the other side

of the same summer street is eating their own cone
under a green awning, and they call for you to join them;

you do and you eat and they eat in silence as it rains
        harder,
and the summer street fills with water; as you finish,

the sun comes out—it is late evening, so the sun floats
on the far side of the flooded summer street—the other

person hasn't quite finished their ice cream cone,
and they offer you the last bite, which you accept,

and it is delicious; now the sun is tired and lying flat
and it is time for you to leave the green awning, so,

without a word, you reach for the other person's hand and
find it already in yours; together, you take off your shoes

and splash through the flooded summer street
toward home. Yes, that is definitely better.

UPON REQUEST

On Lincoln Street in Hartford, I listened
to a Mr. Softee's ice cream truck

endlessly circle the streets to replay
the hurdy-gurdy of its jingle

through nearly every season for three years.
Either too early in the morning or too late

at night, some people chose
to use their car horn instead of a doorbell.

Sometimes, I was awakened
to gunshots fired at four AM.

Here, in this cabin in Cushman, I listen
to the silence after the crickets

have stopped answering the cicadas.
I see the leaves of the sugar maple brighten

to a deeper orange, hay-scented fern begin
to bronze in the sun, and inhale a fragrance

of cinnamon, the scent of their giving up
their lushness for something other.

Anita K. Boyle

MONA'S BOREDOM

When Mona Lisa
came into this life,
she yawned. For weeks
and months, she yawned.
Because she was bored.
Because this life disappoints.
Because of the Tupperware parties.
Because there was no such thing as ice cream.
Because of the cutenesses of bunnies,
kittens, puppies, and polar bears.
Because of the long lines at the grocery store,
at the lunch counter, and even the ducklings
who waddle behind the duck.
She yawned as she grew.
She yawned widely for years.
Because the future was already foretold.
Because water always falls from the tap.
Because there is always someone fighting
in the streets, in the dark, under the moonlight.
Because her boyfriend kissed too hard.
Because flowers are not forever.

But one day,
when she sat thoughtfully
in front of a painter
who painted her big hands,
and her parted hair,
and the folds of her dress,
she happened to smile a little
because of the light above the clouds,

because of the sound of brush on canvas,
because of the painter's humming,
and the empty frame waiting,
and the sudden gasp,
and the permanence
of that moment.

George David Clark

REVEILLE WITH KAZOO

From your overlong, even invincible sleep;
from the pink and orange moth-scales
that collect on your mind like a dust;
from the stately plush where you jonah
in a bottled frigate's belly;
from this lopsided aerie of marigold sheets:
wake up.
    Sleeper, your shoelaces knot
out of boredom. Light wants in your pockets
like money. Wake up from the torpors
of cat fur, from these lingerie dragnets
of lace. The swimming pools
of the future were born this morning
and tenderly swaddled in sun-lust.
Pamphlets announcing new flavors
of ice cream descend on the plaza
in a blitz of sugar. And under the bridge
an angel spray-paints her wings.

BALLET ROUTINE

Curves on a graph controlled by x and y
express acceleration or decline.
But on your hips, what do they signify:
Each muscle winning, losing your design?

Plié, et dégagé, et balancé,
you're at the barre with seven other girls
all beating legs in rhythm as you sway
to strict piano music that unfurls
a private wish to conquer every ounce
of flesh spanning each crested ilium,
each arc held hostage, mute as you all bounce
and stretch your bodies, hurting, healing them.

And then the class is over: time to meet
for pizzas, ice cream cones, across the street.

III Dixie Cup Balm

Age does not diminish the extreme disappointment of having
a scoop of ice cream fall from the cone.
—Jim Fiebig

The train skimmed on softly, slithering, black
pennants fluttering, black confetti lost on its own
sick-sweet candy wind, down the hill, with the two
boys pursuing, the air was so cold they ate ice cream
with each breath.
—Ray Bradbury

I doubt whether the world holds for anyone
a more soul-stirring surprise than the first
adventure with ice cream.
—Heywood Broun

Alice Morris

AS A TINY CHILD "FAILING TO THRIVE"

only when I ate vanilla ice cream

did I see myself
as safely nestled

in a crack
between two worlds

soothed
by a goodness

a reason to stay.

Meg J. Petersen

WHEN THE ICE CREAM MAN COMES

The ice cream man comes every afternoon to the barrio,
pumping out his cheerful tune, (fresa para ti, chocolate
    para mi);
everyone on this dead-end street off Kilometro 12 can
    sing along,
small dark faces look up as he rings his schoolbell, from
    a yellow truck
adorned with smiling white children in their world of
    clean comfort,
free from need. Those children painted on his truck are
    not the sort
he gathers, cause grass wouldn't grow near these houses,
where the water never reaches the taps,
where the mothers and the grandmothers who raise
the sort of children he summons with his pipe organ
    tunes,
often don't have five or ten pesos to press into their
    small hands,
scrubbed clean with harsh laundry soap.
But still he calls them with his seductive music,
like some cream-toned icy pied piper.

It seems so little to ask, a touch of sweetness,
a little cool on the tongue, to kiss away the thick, heavy
air that the fans can only stir in those all-too-rare times
when the electricity arrives, only to depart suddenly,
like a guest long awaited, who leaves too soon. So humid,
breathing feels like swimming, like drowning in air.
        Sometimes

it's worse, when the rains don't come and the batteries
    fail
and lights go out in the middle of the night, stilling the
    fans,
robbing folks of sleep, till they have to lay out on the
    patio in a row,
not touching. At such times, a cool swallow of rum
    raisin
would go down so well. So the women find those coins
somewhere, somehow, so as not to have to sit with all
their children's raw longing for everything they never
    had,
when the ice cream man comes.

Linda Tuthill

DIXIE CUP BALM

I am four years old, trapped in an iron crib
with high bars on the sides.
Nurses skate away, white clouds
moving fast, racing past my tears.

Each morning white coats
gather at the foot of my bed
muttering words like fracture and skull.
I look at their faces, sober as prunes,
and clutch my teddy bear tighter.

Who am I in this high-ceilinged room
with other sobbing children
penned behind tall metal bars?
I want to go home, go home, go home.
When will the bars slide down and my clothes
come back from where they're hidden?

Then Aunt Peg stands in the doorway;
she calls my name: Linda Jane, Linda Jane.

My aunt hands me a cardboard cup
with a tabbed lid.
Today she brings pretty pink!
I take the little wooden spoon
that looks like a paddle, and dig in.
Cold slithers down, comforting
a throat raw from crying.
Strawberry ice cream coats my tongue.
I taste a lick of home.

Bruce W. Niedt

MERCUROCHROME SUMMER

The third time I skinned both my knees
the summer I was eight, my mother
just shook her head. You'll have scabs
on top of your scabs, she sighed,
as she painted them both with Mercurochrome,
that vile red liquid antiseptic that stung
worse than the scrapes themselves.
She eased my pain with a cherry Popsicle,
the sweet and cold in my mouth offsetting
the hot throbbing in my knees. Afterward,
I limped outside and showed Danny next door
my war-painted battle scars, then stuck out
my cherry-stained tongue, and told him
I drank some of the Mercurochrome.
Yuck! he cried.

It was a day full of red: Danny's big sister Julie
sashayed by to show off her new red sundress
and flip hairdo. I told her she looked like Sandra Dee,
but Danny said she smelled like onions. Later,
a fire engine screamed through the neighborhood
when Mr. Berry knocked over his barbecue grill
and set his lawn on fire. Fresh cut grass and charcoal
don't smell so good when they're put together.

I read in my science class that when the sun
goes down, the reds are the first colors to fade.
By dusk, my knees were no longer bright red,
and evening sounds took over for the colors—
the ice cream man on a late run, mosquitoes

teasing my ears, the Fisker brothers setting off
firecrackers in the woods, my parents watching
Jackie Gleason in the living room. I got ready for bed,
pulling my pajama pants over my tender knees,
which were already beginning to heal.

Care Santos
translated by Lawrence Schimel

ELIA IN NEW YORK

There's a place
near Bryant Park
on Sixth Avenue and 42
where Elia,
six years old,
lost a ball of ice cream
that she'd barely tasted.
It took place at one of those
busy crosswalks
where one counts backwards,
from the stop light, threatening
with the worst of a world
of multitudes, hastes
and beautiful cities that no one
stops to look at.
Elia stumbled
and the ball, snowy and sweet,
fell into the middle of that Avenue
that everyone calls Of the Americas.
All New York stopped
in that moment
to listen to the lament of a little girl
as precious as an impossible dream
who had just seen hope
splatter against the burning asphalt.

But Elia looked at the ice cream
as one watches the end of an era,
a chimera melting in the sun,

a nevermore,
a goodbye you,
and cried true tears
that opened a crack, long and straight,
in the hard stone on which
this city of madmen was built,
from the Lower East Side up to 140 street.

Then, Elia looked straight ahead,
forgot the mishap,
thought about the tiniest part
of the good and the bad
that life had to offer her,
classified the matter of that ice cream scoop
in the corresponding place,
determined that it wasn't such a big deal
and started to walk, determined,
toward where the stop light
threatened the apocalypse.

Elia learned to live
a little, or perhaps a lot,
on that Sixth Avenue at 42nd Street,
near Bryant Park
which I can't pass
without remembering it.
I also learned a lesson,
from her look:
that's how it is, Elia said,
how we'll make the future not hurt.

Now, two years later,
that frozen ball melting
under the infernal sun of New York

remains in my memory
and those black eyes that tell me:
when the dream is over,
Mommy,
we always still have
a return ticket to the only thing that matters.

ELEPHANT CUSTARD

At twelve and nine, my brother and I
walked the few blocks
from our grandparents' house
in Margate, New Jersey to the beach,
home of Lucy the Elephant.
This huge hollow elephant-shaped building
used to be a restaurant and hotel.
A window in her leg sold hot dogs, burgers
and soft ice cream the locals called
custard. As a native New Yorker
my understanding of custard
involved eggs and an oven, but this
was lovely, yellow vanilla (pronounced
vanElla) or swirls of chocolate in choice
of sugar or wafer cone dripped down
our chins on a good hot day.
We'd run across the long sand beach
feet burning, to the ocean, wash off
the sweet remnants of our nickel indulgence.

AGE 10

She shouldn't
but she does

allow the dog
to lick

the ice cream cone

dog lick
her lick

dog lick
her lick

vanilla noses
summer love.

Nancy Canyon

OUTDOOR THEATER CHURCH

You and your brother sit in the back seat
of Grandpa's convertible, licking chocolate
ice cream cones. Beezer, the mutt, sits
between you. Grandma reaches a vanilla cone
over the seat, holding it out for the dog.
Grandpa groans, facing the movie screen
where church will be held shortly.
This is the way they do it at Diamond Lake—
cars parked in rows, speakers hooked over
open car windows, just like at night when folks
watch Micky Mouse turn into a magician,
sweeping the floor until brooms and flood waters
multiply, everything going wrong. You worry
about everything going wrong, the things your new
father says: Don't eat too fast and to keep your
elbows off the table. Say: please pass the potatoes
and may I be excused when you've finished
every last bite. But right now, it's just ice cream
on a sunny morning, Beezer lapping up vanilla,
the blank theatre screen waiting for God.

Penelope Scambly Schott

PERSPECTIVE

Drive with care and use Sinclair. 26¢ a gallon.
Under the green Sinclair dinosaur,

the man stuck a stick into oil and wiped the stick
with a blue rag.

In Granddaddy's new Buick, me and my little sister
rode all afternoon,

the road getting longer and skinnier behind us.
My great-grandmother

had disappeared, and nobody bothered to tell me.
How could I learn about history

as everything got farther away?
Granddaddy's pipe smoke bent over and trailed out

the wing window of the car.
The shop where we stopped for rum raisin cones

sold enormous wrapped caramel popcorn balls
tied with a red bow,

but I couldn't have one and soon I'd be too old
to want one.

Or what if the new car crashed and all of us died
right that minute—

Granddaddy's pink head shiny under his fedora
and my poor baby sister

stuck forever at too young to read?

Tim Sherry

ICE CREAM AT CHURCH CAMP

There's no ice in the New Testament.
So standing in line after vespers,
waiting the opening of the snack shop,
the question is so church camp
when someone wonders
if Jesus would have served ice cream
for dessert at the Last Supper
if there had been such a thing in his day.
It's more of the silliness
that sometimes seems so gospel
in the mountains where such questions
are refrigerated most of the year
by ten feet of snow--and deciding
in the heat of a summer evening
which flavor, cone or dish,
how many scoops, is just as important
as answering, *What would Jesus do?*

TWINGE

The dime I stole from her hairpin jar smoldered in my hand—all the way to Mason's ice-cream parlor. The Dixie Cup vanilla treat went down smoothly. I can still taste the wooden spoon.

Harvey Schwartz

WHAT I LEARNED

Can I possibly be the same person I was on Hampden Rd
   where my
black and white world made me feel black and blue
   sometimes?

Row-house images blare at me like Phillies games used to.
Eight-year-old Harvey, full of fury at a cosmic order
spun into disarray when Stan's beat up Good Humor
ice-cream truck stopped at the Fitzpatrick's house
instead of his. He had to blow it up.

He looked past Mrs. O'Donohugh's latest boyfriend
furtively entering her house, Ruth Rubinson scoffing
at Mary Ellen Fitzpatrick playing ball in the street
"after she started to develop," to Big Eddy
Fitzpatrick, six doors down, sleeveless t-shirt, tattoos.
Ice cream truck, big as a barn, stopped amidst beat up
   Chevys and
Fords—randomly parked on the street that we owned—
   where we played ball.

Clean-cut version of the Cory kid would later yell,
"I'm in love with the Marines," when home on leave.

Little Eddy Fitzpatrick staggered up the street like a
   duckling, an hour after
the old man had walked a straighter line. Fitzpatrick's
   crammed in
that row house like a phone booth. I hatched my plan.
Faster than Richie Ashburn diving into third I struck...

Opened the truck hood, turned the radiator cap, poured
    in sand,
knew it would blow up.

Mrs. Fitzpatrick faded into the red heart of her picture
of Jesus. All that blew up was my tiny world, like
red brick chess pieces.

Years later visiting: Big Eddy on the street, I didn't know
if he'd recognize me. "Harvey Schwartz, I thought
    you'd be
an unemployed rabbi by now." Which proved the old man
had a sense of humor and knew more than I thought.

If I'd looked up through sneakers hanging on telephone
wires, ambient light at night and what I didn't know was
    haze,
I might have seen Sputnik yelling a message to me.
"You were lucky it didn't blow up kid. Stand up for your
    rights.
Just don't be such a dumb-ass about what they are."

Susan Roney-O'Brien

TONSILLECTOMY

The doctor screws a pulley into your throat
and hangs a little boat from the cord.
The boat holds a small sharp blade
and when his hands roll back the rope
the knife saws away your tonsils.
Of course you're asleep inside ether,
winding around like a yoyo string,
so all you see is white, all you feel
is air and the sounds you hear
clang under water.

At least that's what the twins next door
told me after I fell asleep
while jumping rope and was sick
all the time. Dad drove me to the hospital
and when I woke, my throat
felt like a scraped knee in my neck.

In the next bed, a boy younger than me
crunched potato chips. The tall, round nurse
bent down and whispered,

You can't have those, but how about
some ice cream? I grinned
and spooned the coolness in.
Then I must have fallen asleep;
I dreamed of long white boats
full of tonsils, pulling out
to dump them in the sea.

MY TEETH
Balanus cariosus (Pallas)

How the mind lands
like a barnacle on certain rocks
holds on, builds its steep-walled
fortress around a body that lies
forever on its back, kicking
food into its own mouth. I found
a box of my old teeth
baby teeth some scrimshawed
with silver fillings others filed
from first bites of apples, ice cream
cones. Also a nickel exchanged
beneath a pillow and one incongruous
fellow thatched at the base and come
from the jaw of a young male elk
my father hunted. Once
at Squirrel Cove he must have tired
of my complaint about a tooth
dangling from its thread of skin
and removed it with the pocket
handkerchief he sometimes spat on
to clean my face as I squirmed
from its intimacy. Long grasses
brown with summer. Ruffled
water swells the cove below. Blue folds
of a kerchief reaching in a child's mouth
toward an amalgamated kernel
that won't let go.

Ann Reisfeld Boutté

A TOUCH OF FEVER

was my ticket to
a day home from school
in my parents' four-poster,
alcohol rubdowns on request,
steaming chicken soup
delivered on a folding tray,
a house call from Dr. Marks,
who seemed able to cure
by crossing the threshold,
an afternoon visit from
Grandma for a game of gin,
"I'm gonna play ya hard,"
she'd warn through her smile,
a freeze on my brother's
teasing and pranks,
a gift from Dad when
he returned from work,
and all the peppermint
ice cream I could eat.

Kelli Russell Agodon

TASTE OF AFFECTION

I am emptying my kitchen
of recipe books, lies
I told to my childhood friends—
My father invented Skybars.
There are so many chocolates I haven't tried.
So many fathers I haven't met
in wide ties, bellies over their pants,
mapping the route to Hershey,
Pennsylvania in '68 Eldorados.
I am busy counting backwards,
subtracting my weight from the day
I learned there wasn't a way to measure
how it feels when two different people
say, I love you. My mother gave me another
scoop of ice cream and told me, I had her
thighs, and my father pouring on
the chocolate syrup saying,
That's why I married her.

Neil Carpathios

THE ONE TRUE WORD

The phone rang as my father sat
eating a bowl of vanilla ice cream
at the kitchen table, picked it up,
put the plastic boomerang to his ear
and listened to the voice on the other
end tell him his mother died moments
ago in Athens, Greece as his face didn't
change except for red on the eyes' rims
and a single diamond weaving its path
down his cheek, then he put the phone
down and said, matter-of-fact, she was
dead—not passed or gone or no longer
with us—but dead—the blunt weight
of the one true word what I suppose
he felt in that instant she deserved
as he left the room to be alone
with the size of his thoughts of her,
I presume, of her body and face and
wrinkled dark skin a million miles away,
wherever she was looking
down from soaring among stars the way
the dead do sprung from the cage
of bones left behind and I stood looking
at the bowl on the table, the spoon fully
submerged where it slipped from his hand
drowning in a creamy ocean of white.

THE ELUSIVE ZEN OF HOUSEWORK

My mother's eyes red from Comet fumes, a cigarette glowed from the corner of her mouth. Dad's armpit-stained, wadded-up t-shirt soaked in a puddle by her bare feet.

From the portable radio, crooner Al Martino pledged his heart.

Mom crouched to scrub inside the refrigerator, its former contents overflowing the trash can.

"What are you doing?" I asked.

"Taking advantage of the blackout," she answered, her cigarette bobbing, ash dropping to the yellow linoleum.

I pointed to an ice cream carton leaking a pool of mint chip. "Can I have some?" I said.

"Go ahead," she said.

I sat cross-legged on the floor, scooping green goo with my fingers, sucking each sticky one clean.

My mother and I stayed quiet for a long while. Life felt good to me. The lesson of the moment—that any bad circumstance could be transformed into a feast, or an opportunity to make things shine.

I did not think then, as a seven-year-old, to ask Mom how she could stand all that housework, the awful fumes, or what went on in her head, as perspiration poured off her brow, her back bent into the rhythmic scouring. All the while, the radio broadcast idyllic love songs.

My mother did not sing, did not even hum along.

Penelope Scambly Schott

YOU, GRIEVING

After the sunlit traffic of bees,
after the chimes of the ice cream truck,
after the calling in of small children,
after the eye of the horse like a gazing-ball
set to reflect the sun-bronzed barn,

let us receive
soft talking on porches,
a breeze rising in the cottonwood leaves,
the sleepiness of regret,
the hand-smoothed sheets.

All these years of loving my dear ones
the best I know how—
patting knuckles, rubbing feet—
and yet, sometimes,
we must allow each other to be sad.

Tom Chatburn

1945 AND HALF PAST TEN

I once sat on the steps

Beside my mother
Who was tall, pretty, and neat,
As the Good Humor Man
In the Ice Cream Truck

Came ringing down the street.
She waved her hand
Like, in Braille, to say
"Don't bother asking,

Your father is off to war
And nothing's the same
As it was before!"
And I remember thinking
On those Germantown

Steps of stone

"So, he got himself

Conscripted,
How come I was being
Restricted

From having an ice cream cone?

(as I watched some
neighbors
getting in line)
I mean, to get one
Only cost a dime!"
Later in life I
would master:
Jacks,
Marbles,
Yo-Yo's,
Double Entry
Bookkeeping,
Tennis,
Pinochle,
And Finally,
Chess—
Oh, and yes, by any
stretch,
The pathway from
child to adult
Is winding,
crooked and rough,
You bet!...
And it's littered
With more than
one thing
I'd like to forget!

Martha Christina

EASY ENOUGH
for Linda

We're nine, holding hands
down Third Street in August,
allowances spent on orange Dreamsicles,
our simple solution to Indiana heat.

My sister and her boyfriend
ride by on his bike,
on their way to the new
Dairy Queen. She's balanced
on his handlebars,
laughing her shrill laugh
and pointing.

After supper she takes me aside,
holds me at arm's length
like something stale
or dangerous, and says we
mustn't hold hands anymore:
people will say we're queer.

Other little girls
our age held hands,
so it was easy enough
to ignore her warning,

and it's easy enough
to call this a love poem
for those two nine year olds,
their dripping Dreamsicles,
their sticky hands.

Jackie Craven

POSTCARDS I WISH I'D SENT LISBETH
WHEN WE WERE GIRLS
AND HER PARENTS SENT HER AWAY

July 8, 1962
The afternoon heats up like an engine.
It revs up the vapor hill,
rips through Mrs. Dooley's hollyhocks,
roars your name with gasoline breath,
and then, at the top of Forsythia Lane,
flops onto Mrs. Emery's lawn,
panting *Lisbeth, Lis—*

July 11, 1962
Don't confuse this gasping day
with the ragged dog Mrs. Emery keeps
tied to her Virgin Mary. He's a sundial
in the grass, spinning silly circles,
yowling at the Good Humor man
who jingles past. Zingos and Lollies
dissolve on my summer tongue.

July 23, 1962
When will you return?
The plaster Virgin sings to me,
but her voice is sugar rough.
The singular vessel of devotion
can't hold our secret words.
Grownup faces peer through
thirsty windows. *Quick,
stop the truck. Jackie needs a
black cow float.*

August 5, 1962

Again today, I hear ice cream toll.
Time turns somersaults over rooftops,
Mrs. Dooley's peonies flutter off
on smoky wings. You melt over the rim
of my frosted cone. Soon you'll fling
your arms around some flea-bitten
boy. You'll forget our special language.

August 19, 1962

Isbethlay,
omecay omehay.
Isbethlay,
arrymay emay.
Marry me forever.

October 12, 1962

Summer is dropping from the hickory tree.
You're a husk carried off by squirrels.
Even Mrs. Emery's dog has forgotten you.
Go ahead, ask him who he loves.
He'll only bark his name:
Ralph! Ralph!

Scott T. Hutchison

ICE CREAM

The carnival is in town. You've odd-jobbed

the dull neighborhood for three hard weeks
planning your crazy move, and have enough money
to try this dating thing. You make
the phone call. There are insect-crawls
beneath your skin, the sweat on your head
at the follicles percolates and geysers. She says yes.

You stroke ten blocks to her house, burning up
the bottoms of your sneakers. Tried counting
the sun-warmed concrete squares to settle yourself,
    became
confused, lost. Birds in the trees singing
or laughing. A summer day has settled into a droning
    level
of just plain hot. Thinking about how you're going to
    knock
and die saying hello to her mother, but your date
is sitting on the stoop, bounds out to meet you saying "hi."

When did she take your hand? Why did that carny smile
and present her with a teddy bear when you threw wide
on all three tries at the milk bottle game? Did the sleepy
    town
grow bigger, the carnival lights brighter, when she
    pointed out
the school and church and people below
and places you never knew the name of
from the top of the Ferris wheel? This girl smells sweeter

than blue cotton candy, her giggles and screams
erase all fear in the Fun House, on the Tilt-a-Whirl.

The evening is cool, the concrete squares are old friends
on the random slow walk home. She has a teddy bear
and a bag of water with a crazed goldfish bearing your
    name
clasped in one hand—the other is occupied
with a mint chocolate chip cone. Her tongue rolls
around the edge, and then she puts it up to your mouth.
You're sharing this with a girl. Your taste buds
are rapturous, calling out halleluiahs
to your electrified skin, the intoxicated top of your head—
maybe it was vanilla before, maybe you can't even
    remember
before, but you know what your favorite flavor of ice
    cream is now,
know you can never—don't want to—go back.

THANKS, FRANK

In 1923, Frank Epperson (ironically?) introduced ice on a stick to firemen, and fifty-five years later, in the heat of the high Sierra desert, with the sophisticated palate of an eight-year-old, I would devour two or four root beer-flavored popsicles. Lip smack with brief satisfaction before I would frantically search the Twin-pop collection for more. Addict—yes. Ashamed—never. Hot days, I still crave them. Though, like all good things that were surely not good for me—men with foppish hair and wild creative streaks, my grandmother's potato salad, and German imitations of Tom Waits—they cannot be found anymore.

Hunter Keough

RECURRENCE OF BEING YOUNG

When I lived on Spottswood, near the college
bookstore and the local bar, I used to sit
in my apartment on "off-days" (sometimes
even during my piano class) to hear the stray

celestial sound of an ice cream truck singing
down Memphis' side streets, soft against
the sirens of firetrucks and heat. I'd sit
and hum nostalgia like an old Southern

hymn, and think how life had changed
        into constant stagnation. Warhead
            ice cream, warhead / warhead;
our youth makes screamers out of us all.

I'd fall asleep to the ice cream jingle similar
to how I took childhood naps—hopeful and alone.
I would doze, content, at the expense of some
knowledge in exchange for greater meaning.

Michael Meyerhofer

THE TIP

I stayed a few days at a casino
back one blustery Christmas
when all the roads and airports closed.

My brother counts cards but I can't
manage anything worse than syllables.
So most of the time, I stayed

in my room or wandered around
and kind of felt sorry for myself.
There was a cheap restaurant

where I'd sit alone and eat,
sometimes staring out the windows
into a near-Siberian parking lot.

One day, though, my view was blocked
by an old man eating ice cream.
He sat by himself, composed

as a Zen monk, spooning neopolitan
past his tan, weathered lips.
He'd already placed a few dollars

and a miniature Babel of loose change
next to the napkin holder.
No wife or grandchildren in sight.

Just his calligrapher's wrist, his spoon
circling that palm-sized dish
again and again until he was done.

IV   Ice Screams

Without ice cream, there would be darkness and chaos.
—Don Kardong

...success is to failure as butter pecan ice cream is to death.
—Rupert Holmes

I love revision. Where else can spilled milk be turned into ice cream?
—Katherine Paterson

POSTER BOY

*A 12-year-old boy soldier was asked what he missed the most
after he was rescued. He said, "When I had a gun I never had
to worry about food."*

Sweet faced boy in a green bandanna.
Hair in his face. Covering his eyes.

His fingers clutch an ice cream cone.
Pistachio. A strawberry on top.

AK 47 leans into him.
He leans into the camera.

The ice cream melting.

Faleeha Hassan
translated by Dikra Ridha

TWO DOVES

Every time my father is late from the Battlefront
sickness strikes my mother
and I tour with her the hospitals of Najaf

I write to him come 'back to us now
Make your sergeant to read my words: I am about to die'

He returns my letter, laughing
'We are the amusement of the blind man'
Oh you River of Jasim, you tore my years
between my father's supposed victories
and my mother's wishes in the emergency room

they used to take care to plant hope in her mind
by sticking on the glass door
two notices that say: (awaiting death certificate)

Her heart ages so fast
I vomit from hearing the chants
Every time the presenter says 'victory is on the
horizon'

My grandmother's eyes rise to the ceiling
she hides a mocking smile

With rage I scream at the screen 'no victory's coming'

She whispers: 'god is generous'
'You sound like my father when I asked for ice cream'
She quietens and we contend
Awaiting his return before a new battle

Fearing that a last fight can end the life of a dove

....
Najaf: an Iraqi city, where the poet was born and lived
    most of her life.
River Jasim: is a river situated between Iraq and Iran,
    the location of many battles during the Iraq/Iran war.

Steve Abbott

I SCREAM, YOU SCREAM

The August afternoon would have embraced hot rivets
        thrown by men walking high steel, but construction
            work
was slow, people taking jobs that kept them from falling

too far. Openings appeared and disappeared like tar bubbles
        in the street, where bits of iron blazed comet tails
of rust toward the gutter. The pavement's heat shimmer

raised a curtain on ninety degrees in the shade and
        the downpress of layoffs and cutbacks, the pressured
atmosphere of a town swimming with people left behind.

Men and women slumped on porches and steps, tank tops
        puddling sweat, the radio mumbling some beach song,
and kids huddled in their rooms in the glow and glare

of digital screens, the world reduced to the palm of a hand.
        A dragonfly's buzz at the screen faded into what seemed
at first a shred of memory, fragmentary until notes took
    shape

as melody, a piper's flute trolling the baked sidewalks and
        growing louder until a white truck turned the corner,
its squared sides a billboard of familiar popsicles,

fudgsicles, bomb pops, push-ups, ice cream sandwiches.
        Behind the wheel, a graying man once a laborer
or warehouseman stared through the windshield,

half-insane with the refrain of eight bucks an hour and endless
    loopings of a steam-calliope version of "Union Maid."
Oh, you can't scare me, I'm sticking with the union.

Janet R. Kirchheimer

TUESDAY AFTERNOON ON THE E TRAIN

A tattooed man sits down
next to me on the E train heading

to 71st and Continental, complains
to no one in particular about

the subway service, the lack of it,
surly MTA employees and rising prices,

waving a chocolate ice cream cone, gesticulating
with it in between swear words.
.
At Queens Boulevard he flashes
the peace sign to those of us who remain,

saying, "I gotta move out of here,"
as the doors open and close.

Diane Kendig

MARIA BLANCHARD'S *EL CARRITO DEL HELADO* (THE ICE CREAM CART)

I had seen this scene as I was meant to, a certificate
on the ground, the crown thrown on top, the fluffy bow
of his white shirt matching the white band of his boater.
His stiff black jacket, the scalloped bowl of vanilla ice cream.
I tried to see what the critics saw in the angle of his arm
against the paving bricks, the romboidalness of it,
as they say in Spanish. It's not the aesthetics got me.

My friend, a nurse, said, "Look at the girl behind the cart,"
and I do, see how I missed her, barely able to stretch
to hold the ledge of the cart. I remember that reach
to the shelf that held suckers at the bank,
to the bookshelf where the librarian waved for me
to get books myself though I was not tall enough to.
Eventually, they were handed down to me by an aunt
who even had *The Scarlet Letter*, whose "A" I could not get.

So I don't mean my reach left me with the nothing
that this girl's does. She has arrived after the boy
and has thrown her cane down on top of his laurels,
would like some sweet herself, holds on with one hand
for support, waves her other hand just above the edge,
but it seems the ice cream man
left the picture once he served the boy whose
back's turned on her, eyes staring further off, blasé,
used to such awards, such treatment and treats.

HOLY, HOLY

"Put the rope of line tightly"
Says my mother
Wrapping it all around.
I am in my mouth a "Goddammit"
As an Ice Cream
but only I say:
"I told You, I said
I'm not talking You anymore."
Then she turns over my face
Giving to me a slap.
I'm looking now my neighbour
Across the window
I love her in the silence.
I'm moving and making sounds
For too she looks at me.
I don't like what my father
Says to my mother
Falling in Love:
"Fucking Whore, love Me"
And she answering:
"Stop yelling, bastard¡"
From head to foot
I love my neighbour
And I dream for to carrying her
Near the old brown tree
Because my blood, red blood
Is now dripping
As the tree's sap.
Look at me
I'm now writing in its trunk

"Holy, Holy, You aren't a Whore
You're a Virgin"
Crawling around
Kissing, kissing the Tree
A temple of Love for me
Where my candle fires
And my wishes glow.
Holy, Holy
If You hear me in silence
Feel free in Your body
With my mind.
I am in You.

Bonnie S. Kaplan

SKID ROW, LOS ANGELES, 4 P.M.

There is screaming in the streets
below, sirens emanate
up seven floors to where I teach.
Every afternoon a crackling

tune draws closer, a relentless
loop of Pop Goes the Weasel.
The Ice Cream Man comes to Sixth
and San Pedro, takes EBT for payment.

They still manufacture Bomb
Pops in striated flavors—cherry, lemon-
lime, and blueberry—summery
sweet, dripping patriotism

all over the veteran's hand,
the one that still works.
Sometimes the Ice Cream Man
brings his son on the route.

The boy helps deliver Good
Humor Bars to those in wheelchairs,
makes change. Grown-ups form
a loose line at the truck's window

for frozen Big Sticks,
Fifty-Fifty Bars, King Cones.
There is laughter and blue tongues
and a woman who thinks the Ice

Cream Man is stealing her thoughts—
the layers of peeling stickers
on his truck are evidence enough,
and how he keeps everyone coming back.

Monique Gordon

BEYOND SCARED

Loud-Mouth warns, "Friday's da thirthteefh!
It's on my phone! Monday's my birfday!
I'm just lettin' you know!"

He's been shot. Jailed. Beaten.
Not one tragedy went down on Friday the 13th.

Next day, homeboys hide inside.
Nature enjoys silent street of the 'hood,
'til voice on ice-cream truck amplifies
over calliope tunes with attitude,
"HEELLO. HEELLO. HELLO."

Seniors sit on stoop sippin'
moonshine from Styrofoam.
They're not scared.

Next day, homeboys sit side-by-side,
shoulder-to-shoulder on stoop, reading phones.
Message reads, "I heard I've been on your mind.
I decided to text you. You don't know jack about Satan.
What you do know about me, will fit into a thimble."

Tamara MC

BARELY THERE

He found me there barely twenty-five
What he didn't know was that in my arms
I still held them: Two brown boys—
Barely four and barely two
I was barely there,
Barely dressed, he swirled me
And I disappeared
Like Caramel Coffee-Mate
Into a Circle K 24-ounce coffee
In four beats, we tapped—
Kicked to the clave
Dile Que No

In the Jardin, I hid behind bushes
As my mom approached
Grabbing my arm, he would fling
Me on his motorcycle, and we
Would ride. I would leave them.
Down windy roads we went,
Me and my *Mexicano* Oscar.
Balloon sellers. Ice cream vendors.
With him, I always ordered coconut *helado.*
With him, I lathered myself in coconut
Cream. I was creamy & cream-ilicious, the cream
He had desired. I became his Creamsicle Popsicle.

I had rented an apartment for the summer,
And he stayed with me,
In my bed. *They* were still there. At night,
At Club Habana, we swayed.

My hips were in constant motion.
During the day, we rode—
To ghost towns, to places girls like me should
Not have been. The mom remained.
Until she left. And then the lady at the
Front desk became the sitter. At 4 am,
We would wave to her. She knew something
Couldn't have been right. Something was wrong.

The sex therapist asked, "What is it about the night?
    About the darkness?"
I answered her truthfully and honestly and said,
    "I don't know."

Kathleen McClung

INSTRUCTIONS FOR CLOSING

No need to panic if you're locked inside.
He takes a special pleasure telling me
the walk-in freezer's safe. No homicide

has happened here. Nobody's even tried
but, say they did, just hypothetically:
no need to panic if you're locked inside.

Just wait, stay cool (ha ha) then, voilà, slide
this lever to the left, which sets you free.
The walk-in freezer's safe. No homicide

or even frostbite, Darling. He takes pride
in orienting each pink-shirted employee.
No need to panic if you're locked inside.

The crackheads only want quick cash, so hide
here with the French vanilla, strawberry.
The walk-in freezer's safe. No homicide.

He lingers, strokes an icy tub, asks if I've tried
an older guy. Diane clocked out at nine thirty.
No need to panic if you're locked inside.
The walk-in freezer's safe, he said. He lied.

Erika Mueller

RAPE

To leave the body is easy.
You don't even have to close your eyes.

Pick an age before. Pick a fireplace
and someone safe in the other room, close by.

Later, the dryer will finish its cycle. The air
will smell of his peppermint gum and Snuggle softener.

Sometimes you'll wonder what was found
in the mummy of you, wrapped tight

somewhere, out of mind. Did you blink? Did you
smell like peach ice cream? You were young

and could've been younger. Too many
tell this story, wrangle it into a corner like a bar stool

to reach that small basement window
that still hovers somewhere off to the right, shining

like a blind cataract in the dark. We
reach up every moment, right now.

We're always about to get out.

Z.G. Tomaszewski

HOSPITALIZED

Soundward
Echo chamber
A minor ringing
in the middle of the afternoon
all afternoon
a foghorn
Rusty gate erring
on its hinges
a starling's static
endures
If you've been singing
into the microphone of night
ice cream melting out of voice
if you've heard
the yawn of a wolf
or dust settle
on a marcescent leaf
then you're close

ICE CREAM

Through the windows
the loud singing of frogs.

Where the cars sleep at night
she continues to flower, expanding as she opens

despite birdshit and white seagull feathers on the floor.
In the morning, blue-purple morning glories

echo in the Indian print bedspread.
A blackbird dive-bombs her,

squawking, claws digging into her scalp,
mistaking her pale hair for straw.

Heat presses down, a sweaty palm.
Wild unruly river, beautiful creature

tumbling toward and away from the road,
leads her to the ocean

where shadows creep among smooth dunes,
interrupting and interpreting the ice cream surface.

Maureen Alsop

CRÈMEÉMANCY
divination by means of ice cream drippings

We believe first in bee orchids. Magenta frangipani or fig.
We taste singing and unfold wax geometries, coral colored
cypress. A kind of speed. Until, soft chaperone, there is no
more to be made of arrangement. Love's witness separates
a soft illogic, a 'we' as emptiness. The battlefield's silent,
as sun's mouth gropes asphalt. We were visions. Ask what
swarms resolve; this was not. The place the dead live.

Alice B. Fogel

CHOICES
including several words and phrases from William Stafford

You and your metaphysical skateboard,
are you encouraging good fortune in your own little ways?
How do you act to make things right when you veer
this way and that around those obstacles
only you find in the otherwise empty park? Lucky you, you
keep things by not having them. In the kitchen of your
    psyche
the freezer is full of ice cream, a dozen glorious flavors
and none edible because not one of them is all of them.
Take heart! Or never mind. Alternatively, try thinking
of amnesia as a form of apology, a lapsed paralysis, a
    stance.
Wisdom tells us we should never make choices
if we can't trust the world. Or is it heroic to be
like the octopus, flipping colors depending on your arc,
wheeling in eight directions all at the same time?

Linda Lancione

NOTE TO MOM

I saw his place today, high picket gate
wide open, a cheap canvas chair
and empty wine jug—sound familiar?—
parked in a sunny spot by the barnlike workshop
he built thirty years ago, its redwood planks
now weathered to a deep russet glow.

No truck, maybe he'd gone for breakfast
at the local café, or to pick up half a pound of nails.
I inched past, not daring to turn in his driveway,
but for miles, driving southward home,
I scanned faces in each passing pickup
for his shrubby beard, gone white.

Out of his range, breathing free,
I started singing in the car. At Stewart's Point,
I stopped for a Dove Bar—our old fave—
chocolate on chocolate, cold sweet comfort.
Your son has a life—I just wanted you to know.
Now, will you let me go?

Judith R. Robinson

THIS SUMMER MOMENT
for Donald Featherstone

Saint James Street
At mid-afternoon.
The sound of traffic.
Wheeling, humming.

A window box
Of orange roses
Outer petals gone pale
In full sunlight.

Down on Fifth
Dangerous numbers
Staggering toe to toe
Bumper to bumper
Along the broken street.

They must work
To collect the fat
To stake the flag
Up the golden pole.
To drag every living thing
From the swift gray river.

The Chinese doctor
Who never speaks
Pulls into the spotty shade
Of his driveway.

CNN reports the father
Of the pink flamingo
Has died.

No more white ice cream
Trucks, very few honey bees.
No more starlit hay rides
Or other glowing events.

Meg J. Petersen

GLASS TULIP SUNDAE DISHES AND DARK SKELETON BONES

The last time I saw you alive and whole and black, in
     Helados
Bon, at the corner of Italia and Independencia, we ate
     bubble gum
ice cream in waffle cones with tiny wooden spoons. I
     steadied
my son on a plastic horse, while you told me you were
     pregnant,
by a grey-haired German to whom you had been
     teaching Spanish.
I remember how your hand trembled as it gripped the
     spoon, stabbing
at the odd dessert, so impossibly blue. Yet your eyes
     were still. Outside,
a public car backfired, and you jumped, as if it had been
     a gunshot.
I too felt the danger, a ragged disquiet darkened the
     day, as a heavy cloud
eclipsed the Caribbean sun. Born in Sabana Grande de
     Boya, the year after
the revolution, you have always emerged from ruins,
     from the darkness
of nights in the campo without luz, from precariousness
     and peril.
But I had never known you afraid.

He arrived that day, the gruff German man in a silver
    car, who chauffeured
you away through rain-drenched streets, into the life
    that erased you.
People say money makes you whiter, but I didn't believe
    them until we met again,
years later, at Baskin Robbins in Bella Vista. You had
    changed your name,
reverting to one you had never used (perhaps "Marta"
    seemed more German).
Your hair, straightened into the costly wave of the finest
    salons, hair a breeze
can lift, gently shaped your somehow lighter-complexioned
    face. You had become the wife
of a man who lived on another continent, become a person
    who hired servants,
who raised a light-skinned daughter with an odd German
    name. I studied hard
to find traces of you: in your mouth, your dark eyes, the
    way your lips pulled
into a smile. Gazing at you in all your prosperity, as you
    delicately spooned
coconut ice cream from a bright pink cup, I thought how
    sometimes danger doesn't threaten,
but arrives instead in a luxury car, bearing gifts too rich
    to refuse.

The next time we met for ice cream, in Maniquí Restaurant,
    Plaza de la Cultura
as we ate mint chocolate chip from glass tulip sundae dishes
    with long handled spoons,
you had grown more pensive. Your daughter had entered
    university, and emptiness
seemed to pursue you. You reminded me about the first
    time you visited
my country, long before you met the German man, how you
    arrived in the bitter cold
of a rare snowless New Hampshire January; and you told me
    again how you cried in grief
for the trees, how their branches, bare and desolate like
    dark skeletons' bones,
knocked against the winter sky, made you long for the
    verdant beauty
of your island. Even now, you told me, all these years later,
you can't forget their stark loneliness, or their
    overwhelming
sadness. "You don't understand," I told you, my voice
    half-pleading,
"It was only for a season; they were only waiting.
They will come back,
rich and lush and strong."

Thom Schramm

WAKE: 1978

Maybe it's an urban myth
that the ice cream man comes with
drugs up his sleeve, crack and speed
in packets with lick sticks, beads
of ecstasy on necklace strings,
yet she hears the truck coming
from three blocks away, tosses
her books into the long stalks
of timothy and yellow
poppies along the walk, throws
her head back, then sprints home
to beg for another loan
until allowance day.
She enters the house crazed,
shouting. They all understand.
Everyone sits holding hands
beside the uncovered
box in which her brother
lies. She looks to his eyes
but can't see behind
the coins they placed in the way
to shield her from his blood-shot gaze
the eyedrops couldn't polish off.
She reaches for the coins in awe—

1994

The last time I saw my friend he was sleeping in the living room, and a Beethoven piano sonata was playing. He was thirty-six and dying of AIDS, and he had contracted a virus that destroys the part of the brain that controls motor responses, such as breathing and swallowing. He still enjoyed music. I sat beside his bed and spoke into his good ear. His speech was slurred. He dove for air and huffed out words. It was difficult. I drew an alphabet board so he could point to letters, and I asked what was on his mind. He spelled, "I don't feel cheated." Then he spelled, "I wish I had written more," as if to say he had cheated himself. I said, "Every writer thinks that." He wanted ice cream. I brought him a Dove bar from the freezer, and he slurped it hungrily. It dripped on his hands, and I wiped them with a cloth. I thought how alive we are until almost the moment we are not. I said, "You have inspired love in your odd, shy way. How do you explain it?" His smile was lopsided. He said, "I'm not demanding."

3:00 AM THURSDAY
IN THE BELLAGIO COFFEE SHOP

She's ordered a sundae.
Her tongue teases the peak

onto a dome of royal fudge.
In the napkin holder's chrome

I see myself
distorted—a man

with a rudderless lust,
intent on sitting beside her

on the hotel bed,
untying her ribboned hair.

So I crank my brightness
up a notch and go

incendiary. Hello
infidelity. Hello

to her skin
so pale it doesn't

belong in nature.
I touch her hand,

as if it were a spoon
dropped. She fingers

the filigree cross on the chain
around her neck.

What is God
wanting from her now?

Faleeha Hassan

I'M CRYING

Not because you squeezed my heart
and threw it like a sponge into desert,
Yes, I'm crying but not because you did not smile at me
but your teeth look whiter than white when you saw
a woman's shadow pass you,
Yes, I'm crying but not because you are completely healed
and no longer need my whisper to sleep,
Not because you dedicated all the poems you wrote to me
To another woman and she stupidly believed you,
I'm crying but not because I threw my pillow
and I will be Watchful all my life without you,
Yes, I'm crying deeply
because the Ice cream has melted before I got home
and I didn't enjoy eating it.

Tim Vincent

SONNET Á LA MODE

I'm in a supermarket parking lot
In a drab inner-suburb near Pittsburgh
It's raining and shopping carts are sliding
Wet litter swirls in the late-summer heat
I should get home before the ice cream melts
But I'm busy sending text messages
With the engine running and wipers on
Clouds of words above a ruined planet
That the little Frenchman could see coming
Jean Baudrillard's hyperreality
Rivers of words that wear down the mountains
Forests of words that cut away the trees
Life itself a mask, a simulacrum
Beneath which lies nothing, a ravaged face.

Vincent Peloso

WHERE ARE YOU NOW, ELIZABETH DOSS?

Newly married, counting our pennies,
living on student loans and minimum wage,

we stood in the supermarket aisle debating,
"Ice cream or hamburger? Ice cream or hamburger?"

With no television, few records or books,
we read every piece of mail received

just for the stimulation,
inventing stories about each anonymous plea

for money we did not have.
In the picture that fell from the envelope,

you were young, thin and barely clothed,
wide-eyed, brown-skinned and haunting.

The letter claimed you would write back
if we only pledged a few dollars.

We didn't. We couldn't. But we never forgot.
When I give to charity today,

it's your pleading eyes I see.
Where are you now, Elizabeth Doss?

Are you still alive? Still poor? Still thin?
I hope you are happy, have found more clothes

and all the ice cream you ever wanted.

V Cravings

Everything was chocolate ice cream and kisses and wind.
—Francesca Lia Block

Never trust a skinny ice cream man.
—Ben Cohen

The only emperor is the emperor of ice cream.
—Wallace Stevens

Kristina England

DID YOU KNOW

that ice cream began as flavored rice
and milk, made in China, no labels
back then to shock us into buying local,
no thought of calories or freeing the fat.
No one asks how ice cream is made
these days. No one asks about the cows,
farmer, restless, hungry factory workers
filling cardboard containers with treats.
We do not look inside the box to find
its history. We buy to indulge, to let
the gooey sugar melt in our mouths—
peanut butter, maple walnut, pumpkin,
vanilla bean, blueberry sweet cream—
to escape the dull taste of our production
line lives, sealed up by jobs, marriage,
kids, the desire for something new.

MELTING POINT

I taste my own sweat as I turn
the crank faster, skin sweet with salt
ache. Cream becoming firm. Picnic
work. A reunion of spoons waits

while away at far Poles the sea washes
glaciers no summer remembers. Moon's
bright handle broken on a newly naked

shore. Salt lowers the melting point
but no one makes ice cream
the old way anymore. Seals puzzle
an acid sunset. There are beaches

even sea-salt can't save. Too many
flavors. Too few recipes. I continue
my small, defiant struggle with an old pine

bucket. Someone adds vanilla. Another more
muscle. Those in line with empty
bowls take only what they need.
The simplest science.

Joan Mazza

CREAM

This is what rises, thick layer on top
of thin bluish liquid in the bottle.
Sweet and slippery on the tongue to gobble
down with coffee or whip to peaked fluff
with powdered sugar. This is the best part,
separating on its own, knowing its place
in design, fat and happy, no disgrace
to mix, enhance the culinary arts
of desserts with chocolate or white rice.
Here's what makes quiche rich,
and hot soups smooth.
Shake it to make it butter or turn it to ice
cream sprinkled with nuts. A treat to soothe.
Begin with this instruction from within
to rise! Rejoice at being thick, not thin.

GELATO

She buys me gelato,
my favorite,
buts eats it
on the way home.
It was so cold, so delicious,
coffee sweet cream,
I'm so sorry,
she says with a kiss,
and hands me
the empty dish.

Susan J. Erickson

IF I WERE A CUP OF CONCUPISCENT CURDS

I'd seduce your lips
and whitewash your throat
with promises we both know
melt in an afternoon.

When I am emptied
leave mute gladiolas
at the foot of the bed.
Leave me for the cat
with her indecent tongue,
leave me for the washers
with their opalescent suds.

Tara Betts

LISTENING TO RAEKWON'S "ICE CREAM"

A revved up piano loop rotates
Earl Klugh's "A Time to Love"
into tinkling ice cream trucks,
except one emcee stands on
a white truck and swings
his walking stick and recites
the familiar hook over beat.

Each series of rhymes tries
to woo a girl from around
the way who must always
remain cool, uninterested.
Even then, don't be thirsty
was a rule, another emcee
asks if her name is Erica,
calls her Black Miss America,
right, true? She offers a smirk.

Other women dance around
the truck in white ringer T's
with black trims, emblazoned
with curved capital W's, above
the letter turned symbol, each
woman is a flavor—French
Vanilla, Butter Pecan, Chocolate
Deluxe, even Caramel Sundaes.

What woman, who wants to be
cherished and whole, would be
edible, sweet, and object.

What woman wouldn't want to be
wanted, held, savored, licked and
called sweet, if one chooses to be.

Kaaren Kitchell

THE WOLF

Elizabethans called it The Wolf,
that hunger that ravens past
the point of satiation.

We were far from our families,
from any semblance of normal (if such exists),
no boys around (if such were your taste),

little of what makes life sweet
for young teen girls. But
we had games and contests.

It was one block away from school.
Each scoop had a rounded head
with a little rim around it:

Love Potion #9, Wild and Reckless Sherbet,
French Vanilla, Rocky Road—
31 in all. I won.

O, creaminess! O, satisfaction!
O, the body filled full!
O, drunk on the sweetness!

It would have to do
until I found
what it was meant to replace.

ICE CREAM SECRETS

So childlike,
I wrap my tongue around

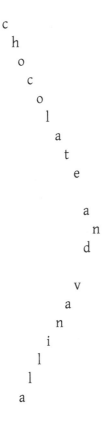

swirls, savoring the
sweetness to come
that is you.

THE FERRY LINE

That was the moment
he knew he loved her.
Dodging minivans,
cars, pickup trucks
in the ferry line,
double fisting triple scoop
blackberry ice cream cones.
Purple trickles ran
between her bare fingers, flicked
into the summer heat,
dotting windshields, side mirrors
as she ran toward him.

He'd taught her how to ride a bike.
Really ride, clipped in
pedaling light, fast
up the island's hills,
flat out down.
Now he watched her
finish off her cone,
bike balanced on hip,
lick her sticky fingers,
rub them clean on her bike shorts,
lean on her pink handle bars,
look at him with that smile.

Ali Znaidi

TINY BITS OF PLEASURE

Smooth solid foam lingers in
the sheltering display of the cone.

The sun cannot shake the freezing breath
of the layered cream conglomerate.

Water begins to take different shapes
in her mouth.—Tiny bubbles longing for pleasure.

Lusty smiles painted upon her lips
conceal aphrodisiac thoughts.

This lust resists the agents of destruction
through freeing every bit of ice cream into her mouth.

—Constructing other worlds of possibilities
beyond the margins...

Gail Braune Comorat

TWO-WAY CONVERSATION WITH
THE ICE CREAM MAN

We never talk about the weather or politics or even
world peace. He and I speak in flavors, whisper

sweet somethings: Chocolate Chip Cookie Dough,
Oatmeal Cookie Chunk, Half Baked.

My ice cream guy is earth-friendly, churns eco-flavors
like Rainforest Crunch and Fossil Fuel, serves me

only from recycled containers. I adore this man
clad in white, splotched with rainbow samples

from his frozen buffet. We love to debate
the finer merits of sticky toffee pudding, cinnamon

dulce de leche, and caramel cone. We spoon,
we sample from every bowl while flaunting

our coolness, our good taste. He gives thanks
for Vermonty Python; I delight in Cherry Garcia.

Together, we get lost in Moose Tracks and Turtle Soup.
I suffer brain freezes from bingeing on too much

Chubby Hubby, too much Chunky Monkey
while he serenades me, breaks out oldies but goodies

like Hunka Burnin' Fudge and Bohemian Raspberry.
We'll stick together, my man and I, forever singing

dulcet duets of Cinnamon Buns and Peppermint
Schtick. Time will melt around us,

our cozy windows will frost and crystallize
from our many pleasured sighs.

Nancy Scott

THE GOOD HUMOR MAN, 1960

Dorothy's dating the Good Humor Man
but we're gorging ourselves
on fudge ripple sundaes
smothered in gobs of whipped cream.
Sometimes I crave the real stuff, she says,
not stored in his truck for months.

She complains he brings her
torpedo pops or almond crunch bars
when what she wants is red roses.
(or maybe it's because
he's got six toes on each foot)

He's part of an illustrious history, she says.
Ice cream has been around 3000 years.
Is that so? I wonder where this is going.
Marco Polo discovered it in China.
Montezuma poured hot chocolate over it.
Dolley Madison was famous for
her frozen pink cream.

I'm licking my spoon as she prattles on.
When great grandma was a child,
the Hokey Pokey Man stood on a corner
yelling, *a penny for a lump*, instead of
jingling those crazy bells
and tooling around in a truck.

Why persist with the history lesson?
By now, the rest of her sundae is soup.
It's the toes.
Yes. It's got to be those twelve toes.

Dana Beardsley Crotwell

UNDERSTANDING

I knew my husband loved me when
he went to Ralph's and asked why they
stopped making my ice cream.

Then he emailed corporate and they told us they
"we're going in a new direction"
but stores might still have some left.
So he drove to all surrounding so-named groceries
and found the last two cartons of Tiramisu and
he put notes on them in the freezer, "mom only."

I rationed out the coffee cream with
fudge rivers, dark chocolate pieces and
imitation rum flavoring
until the miniscule
amount left was completely covered with ice crystals,
and I finally threw the last carton
in the trash
and admitted the truth.

I would find another flavor
but would definitely keep the husband.

ICE CREAM CRAVINGS

When a particular flavor digs into you, and
the craving explodes to a daily fix—
when you must have that strawberry malt

every night after dinner—drive to the Carvel
stand the next town over, do your personal
satisfaction inventory—did I get my quota?

Which is of course, a non-dimensional quantity,
it's a tongue-feel, a throat index measure
it cannot be weighed on a scale or doled out

it must come in a tall glass or a bottomless
pint. Oh, the rimmed fantasy of that last sip
when the suck of the straw is loud

intrusive, the lick round the edge of the glass
to catch the foam bubbles carrying the
flavor of time, those days, that year or two,

however long it took for the withdrawal.
I once had it bad for a praline caramel swirl,
once for Ben & Jerry's chocolate with black

and white cows, dense chips to chew. Days
we indulge such cravings, forego health
recommendations, let the tongue, and the mind

insist their way, our right to each luscious bite.
One time it took the store closing down to stop
my nightly wanderings, like a sleep walker

compelled I trekked to satisfy my fix, even
today with frequency there are journeys
I'll make for ice cream and ice cream alone.

SELFIE-KUS

1
    up close
and hawt in the hotel

bathroom.   pouty
            handtowels.

2
we laugh at
my ice cream
            melting—some
girls
        out, just
        shopping.

3
at the frat party.
  beerpong,   muscle
                        shirts,
lots and lots of
tongue.

4
aren't these
flowers—white blossoms
against white
lace—
just
   just perfect.

5
lol. stereotypical
                    bootypic.

        does this dress
            make me?

6
black lipstick.
                    this is my first
            duck face
            post.

7

                me and the bff

                    under sunshine
            and big hats—
                falling out,
    happy.

8
morning
  in the kitchen.
 beautiful

window.
it's not me
            again.

9

        fashionistas—soft
lighting
            turns us
            chai-latte
       timeless.

Joan Leotta

INDIANA ICE CREAM TREAT

My blue *Volare* flew
like a fallen piece of
sky along the path
made by country
roads overhung with
tree limbs supporting
curtains of red, orange, and
yellow leaves.
At last I reached IU.
After hugs and a walk,
my cousin and I
took off for a burger lunch.
Rounding the corner
near her dorm, we were nearly
past the Campus Creamery when she
exclaimed, "Oh dear, Creamery closes for
the season in just an hour."
We made a U-turn,
deciding ice cream before burgers.
Soft vanilla goodness
soon spiraled from stainless steel
into two funnel cake cones.
We sat amid the leaves
at the outdoor tables
watching the creamery close-up
and gazing occasionally at the road.
Suddenly a VW "bug"
balancing a burger on its roof
screeched around the
corner. The bug bumped the curb.

That plastic burger snapped
off and rolled to a stop in
front of our table.
We laughed as we inspected
faux lettuce, tomato,
burger and bun
"Glad we had dessert
first," my cousin said.
"This burger's overdone."
I agreed, and finished my cone.

Joanne M. Clarkson

SWEET DEMONS

Cannibal at 2 a.m., I hunt with rusted spoon
need as deep as a vestigial heart. Hunger
has little to do with this tryst. Everyone

is asleep. Everyone in my whole world
including my stronger self. Only this insatiable
ghost drifts through shadow, called

by a sweetness so irresistible I risk dress
sizes and blood vessels of a jittery
pulse to taste, taste, taste, not eat

so much as devour a quart, a half-
gallon: Rocky Road, Neapolitan, Triple
Fudge, Butter Pecan. Consoling cream

buzzes my parting lips, duels my tongue. Tingles
my teeth. The swallow so potent
I shiver. I do not stop until the carton

collapses. Then search for more shoving aside
frozen peas and hamburger carefully labeled
by death date. Afterwards

I feel no orgasm but shame. My tears are
icy. Pleasure never lasts. No memory
of the French vanilla kisses of this transient

lover. Only gifts to return. I lock
the bathroom door. Everyone is sleeping.
The mirror is dark.

Karl Elder

DEATH BY CHOCOLATE

Sweet. Delicious. Deliberate.
Earned not in the conventional fashion
but from a carton
with an ice tea spoon
and a brand of ice cream
from a regional dairy in the heart of Wisconsin.

Contrary to what you may imagine,
the victim takes on
no new complexion, pallor,
nor pounds. The face remains
the body's face, surprised
should it catch a glimpse of itself
in the reflection of spoon
and not another self
in this slow death called
the life.

Yes, this is the life:
Exercise each morning. Abstinence.
And sex in the afternoon, calories spent,
that one may feast by evening,
oblivious to which channel,
which batter, which inning
in what city, which trial, which riot,
which approaching storm—
yes, as if by candlelight,
this take-out in your lap,
then crème de coco for desert.

Later, should ever you not
kiss your love goodnight,
let it be not chocolate
you forgot
but appetite.

Nancy Pagh

OVEREATER SESTINA

Strawberry ice cream
Barbeque potato chips
Nothing hits the spot
But devour
(Sorry)
Atkins' diet tomorrow

Start fresh tomorrow
Rocky road
I'm sorry
Cool ranch Doritos
Devour devour devour
Nothing finds the spot

Cannot fill that spot
Grapefruit diet tomorrow
I devour
New York super fudge chunk
Pringles sour cream
I'm sorry, sorry

Abjectly sorry
Nothing seems to reach the spot
Cheezy popcorn, blue corn tortilla chips
Eat nothing tomorrow
Chunky monkey
I devour

Devouring
Sorry
Vanilla

Empty spot
Try tomorrow
Lays

Super nachos with guacamole
Devouring me
Maybe tomorrow
I'm sorry, I'm sorry
The spot, the spot
Cherry Garcia

Maple walnut ruffles
the spot devours
sorrow tomorrow

Marilyn L. Taylor

A HIGHLY CALORIC LAMENT

A pox upon you, Charlie's Chili Dogs,
T.G.I. Friday's, Coldstone Creamery,
you harpies of the dreaded calorie—
quit hitting on me till my judgment fogs,
and every vein and capillary clogs
with drippings from your latest recipe!
Arugula? Not for the likes of me,
and neither are those dreadful diet blogs.
Been there, done that-- gave all my sweets away,
ate naked salad, kept the flab at bay.
But nowadays my magnitude increases.
I'm getting tubby. Fatter by the day.
Just look at me: mine aft has gang agley,
my life's in shreds, my mind's in Reese's Pieces.

Carol Levin

ELEGY TO VOWS

Sang a ceremony with divine unction
vowing exclusively flowers
of broccoli, green
peas on plates, radish & romaine.
Palatable as biting
into the twang
of a broken fiddle string.

No, I don't eat that way.
Embracing the spirit
of a tambourine
drumming and jingling, I
tap, heels sing along
with clicking castanets
crossing the kitchen
in pursuit

of a full freezer,
creamy French Vanilla.
Holding the last
note as long as time
I suck the scoop
forsake my vow
I eat it all.

BURY ME

... peppermint ice cream ... perfect
dessert through the holiday season ...

Dear Dreyers, I'm standing in the kitchen digging
down a half-gallon of your swirled pink with
a serving spoon at 3:00 a.m. Red and green
peppermint candies devil me like full moons. Sweet
cream humors my nighttime melancholy.

Dear Dreyers, I beg you: offer it in March,
April and May. Rejuvenate Easter, Mother's Day
and Father's Day too. I'll crunch candy nubs,
slowly suck them from my teeth.

Dear, dear Dreyers in July, on the 4th,
mint me. By September tingle my throat
as I rest loving Labor Day licking
spoons watching the season wane.

My tiny fridge can't hoard a year's supply.
I could entreat friends with immense freezers
but, Dryer's dear, I'd never see it again.

Peppermint only at Christmas? Please,
Dreyers, be brazen. Feed me Christmas
ice cream all year every year to the last
inevitable day, then, bury me
under a mound planted in mint.

Shoshauna Shy

ICE CREAM SANDWICH IN SPANISH

The whole time on the FreeStrider,
all I thought about were ice cream sandwiches.
Not the rectangular kind in blue packaging
with the perforated wafers that taste
like cardboard, and not the crusty ones
the Good Humor man should have sold
a week ago, and especially not the Oreo
cookie type so dark a brown, you can't
help suspect ink was used to dye them.
No, what consumed me was a chocolate chip
cookie vanilla ice cream sandwich rolled
in dark mint shavings from a certain
corner cafeteria on Knickerbocker Street
that I visited during office lunchbreaks
every Friday while pregnant for the first time.
I would have eaten more of them except
I didn't want my baby to bounce out of me
big as a beach ball and saddled
with a sweet tooth.
Despite this forced boycott six days
a week, I loved the phrase *with child*
and how my body worked to manufacture
a new person with no mindful assistance
from me, and how my Spanish neighbor,
who I ran into at the resale shop, laughed
over the pajama rack *Now you belly-up*
to the table of life!
And while my son has no appetite
for desserts; could take or leave chocolate
in any form, I've gone back to eating

ice cream sandwiches whenever I please,
stationing one in a bowl beneath Bing
cherries, then drenching this with Hershey's
syrup to further soften the dough

and as I slip into "cool down" mode
these last four minutes, I believe that anyone
convinced my habit is unhealthy and should
be overcome, never nursed a baby
with a *sándwich de helado*
melting on her tongue.

SUGAR BABY

I went to the bank and asked to borrow a cup of money.
They said, What for? I said, "I'm going to buy some sugar."
  —Steven Wright

I.

I came with a note from the nuns explaining
I was "fussy and wanted to be held." They also
mentioned giving me Karo Syrup for constipation.

II.

When I die, you will find candy wrappers under
the front seat of my Jeep. Please, cut them in strips,
braid the bright colors into a bracelet called Almond
Joy, Butterfinger & Heath. Attach it to my ankle.

III.

What you need to know is she and I were tethered by
sweets. In the end, they said, *eat anything—*
pie, pudding, cobbler and cookies.

IV.

Her last supper: a strawberry/vanilla swirl
Dixie Cup. She glared when I offered the
tiny wooden spoon. She wanted big bites.

Rodney Torreson

THE DIRTY LOOK I GET AT THE
ICE CREAM STAND

I deserve, not for parking one car over from the car
the basset hound is in, with its fast-beating tongue
and sporting a spangled kerchief,
or for smiling while that tongue practices
for ice cream by clouding white the window
on the driver's side while its master, late 40s,
in a pink pantsuit stands in line,
and turning from time to time, smiles back calmness
while the rick-rack of skin that lines the dog's mouth
is shiny wet with anticipation—

the dog ready for a cone of its own, I am thinking,
while its master will chew on a second one, but, no,
she returns with just one cone, a big one
already looking like a castle melting,
she smiling like a bridesmaid at her canine friend.
And here is where the dirty look is earned:
she opens the car door, and the hound by its long belly
slips down into the foot well
and scrapes its way out onto the asphalt,
and instead of helping, I watch, laughing
as she clutches in one hand the basset hound
and with the other hand herding
and both knees acting as a brace, with much difficulty
boosts it back up into the car, all the while
balancing the cone so the ice cream doesn't topple out—

the lady and dog sitting close together now and I
looking over every five seconds catch the lady
in a pink pant suit sneaking her dog big sloppy licks,

then takes the cone back for some powerful
licking of her own, back and forth over
and over with her tail-wagging pal, while I verify it all,
stepping out of the car and nonchalantly
as I can swinging my head down
to catch in flux that happy tongue
and that's when the dirty look puts a lock on me.

THIRTEEN WAYS TO LICK AN ICE CREAM CONE

1. **Shy**: Go gently, with small licks around the cone, working around the sides and then to the top; don't startle your cone or yourself.

2. **Curious**: Taste in gentle laps around the edges and top, observe and notice, go slow. Be the cone.

3. **Simple**: Start just above the sugar cone, making diagonal swaths up and across the top of the ice cream. Go efficiently around all sides to stay ahead of the drips.

4. **Rustic**: Press your tongue hard against the side, allowing the ice cream to melt slightly against it. Do the same with the top. (Best in a Ford pickup.)

5. **Admiring**: Before beginning, gaze lovingly at your cone, appreciate it as a statue, a monument erected in the name of sugar. But proceed before your monument begins to melt and shrink.

6. **Military**: Charge your tongue up the sides of your cone. Gain the summit. Dominate the cone. Take no prisoners.

7. **Considerate**: Lick your cone when it begins to drip.

8. **Dramatic**: Bite the side of the ice cream and the sugar cone. Keep nipping and biting until it's done.

9. **Sucky:** You're a shopvac. Suck the whole thing in until it's gone.

10. **Teasing:** Slowly and with intention, drop your mouth over the top of the cone. Take your time running your tongue gently around the top, then proceed down to the rest.

11. **Aggressive:** Take the whole ice cream scoop in your mouth until it melts.

12. **Imperialistic:** Eat the whole thing in one bite. Don't apologize.

13. **Brazilian:** With your tongue, lick stripes up either side of the cone, leaving the middle to melt by itself.

Philip Wexler

GELATO

He cradles a single
white paper cone.

Half mango—hers,
half lemon—his.

White plastic spoons,
scoops tiny

as fingernails.
Delicately, they lap

their portions,
she more slowly. One

swallow, then another,
making a game

of respecting the border.
Finishing the lemon,

he encroaches
on her mango,

smacks his lips
at the ripe taste.

Her face radiates
mock amazement.

The spoon slips
from her hand.

She loops her arm
through his.

He finishes
everything left.

M.S. Rooney

YEARS AGO,

on a still and humid January afternoon
in downtown Lima at a café
set beside a swirl of wide streets
by my brother's small apartment
I watched a bearded man
in a wool suit and bowler hat
eat ice cream.

I drank Pilsner from the bottle
and stared, drawn by the way
he closed his eyes, by the way
he smiled to himself, by the way
he wrapped his mouth around the spoon
with a quiet, a private abandon
I envied with more than all my heart.

Debra M. Fox

sudden downpour—
the ice cream truck's jingle
vanishes

AUTHOR BIOGRAPHIES

Steve Abbott edited the poetry anthologies *Cap City Poets* (Pudding House, 2008), featuring work by 74 central Ohio poets, and *Everything Stops and Listens* (OPA Press, 2013), a selection of work by members of Ohio Poetry Association. His work has appeared in journals including *Connecticut Review, Birmingham Poetry Review, Plainsongs, Wind*, and *Spoon River Poetry Review*. He says, "Jeni's Splendid Ice Creams in Columbus are so cool they give other ice creams freezer burn."

Kelli Russell Agodon is a poet, writer, editor, and essayist. She's the author of six books, most recently, *Hourglass Museum* & *The Daily Poet: Day-By-Day Prompts for Your Writing Practice*. She is also the cofounder of Two Sylvias Press where she's an editor and book cover designer. Kelli has fond memories of "Ice Cream Night" as a child where everyone in the house got to eat ice cream in bed, including her dachshund. www.agodon. com/www.twosylviaspress.com

Maureen Alsop, Ph.D. is the author of four full collections of poetry including *Mantic, Apparition Wren, Mirror Inside Coffin*, and *Later, Knives & Trees*. Her poems have appeared in numerous magazines including *Kenyon Review, Tampa Review, New Delta Review, Typo*, and *Barrow Street*. Her favorite ice cream is Gold Medal Ribbon!

Sandra Anfang is an award-winning Northern California teacher, poet, and visual artist. Her poems have appeared in numerous journals. A chapbook, *Looking Glass Heart*, was recently published by Finishing Line Press. Sandra loves Salted Caramel ice cream above all others, though she used to bike miles to Bischoff's for coffee chip as a child. She is a California Poet-Teacher in the Schools and founder of a monthly poetry series in Sonoma County, California.

Lana Hechtman Ayers is a poet, novelist, publisher, and time travel enthusiast. She facilitates generative writing workshops, leads private salons, organizes manuscripts for poets, and teaches at writers' conferences. Lana remains traumatized by a trip to Hershey, Pennsylvania at age five when her mother refused to allow her to have an ice cream cone while the rest of the family indulged. To assuage the pain she eats ice cream whenever she can, even for breakfast.

Tara Betts is the author of *Break the Habit* and *Arc & Hue*. Her chapbooks include *7 x 7: kwansabas* and *THE GREATEST!: An Homage to Muhammad Ali*. Betts earned her MFA at New England College and her Ph.D. in English at Binghamton University. Tara grew up in Kankakee, Illinois, where the creator of Dairy Queen came up with the idea for the popular chain. One of her favorite ice cream flavors is Daiquiri Ice.

Heather Bourbeau's fiction and poetry have been published in *100 Word Story, The Citron Review, Cleaver, Duende*, Francis Ford Coppola Winery's Vendetta Wine Chalkboard, *Nailed, Open City*, and *The Stockholm Review of Literature*. She was nominated for a 2015 Pushcart Prize, and her first collection of poetry, *Daily Palm Castings*, profiles people in overlooked professions. In Reno in the late 70s, her brother introduced her to Jamoca Almond Fudge, for which she was very grateful.

Ann Reisfeld Boutté is a writer of poetry, essays and feature stories. She has a master's degree in journalism and has worked as a feature writer for a daily newspaper and a national wire service. She was selected four times as a Juried Poet in the Houston Poetry Fest. Growing up, her favorite ice cream flavor was peppermint for its luscious pink shade, just the right sweetness, and the infusion of slivers of peppermint candy.

Janet Bowdan can ask for ice cream in five languages and is working on translating "with fudge sauce." She fell in love with her husband when he ordered a mini-sundae on their first date. Her poems have been published in *APR, Best American Poetry 2000*, and elsewhere. She teaches at Western New England University and lives with her husband, son, and a stepdaughter or two in a valley of dairy cows and ice cream stores.

Anita K. Boyle loves ice cream, especially during movie intermissions at home. Favorites? Nestle's Chocolate Chip Cookie Dough and Drumstick. But, she thinks Vanilla Bean is extremely versatile and enjoys it with anything from peaches to espresso. She publishes handmade books filled with the work of Washington State poets through Egress Studio Press. She lives in Bellingham, WA.

Gayle Brandeis is the author of a memoir, *The Art of Misdiagnosis*, a book of poetry, *The Selfless Bliss of the Body*, the novels *The Book of Dead Birds* (winner of the Bellwether Prize), *Self Storage, Delta Girls*, and *My Life with the Lincolns*, and a women's writing guide, *Fruitflesh*. Gayle's dad always used to say, "You can't look sad eating ice cream."

Shirley J. Brewer serves as poet-in-residence at Carver Center for the Arts & Technology in Baltimore, MD. Recent poems appear in *Barrow Street, Poetry East, Slant, Gargoyle, Comstock Review*, and other journals. Shirley's poetry chapbooks include *A Little Breast Music*, 2008, Passager Books, and *After Words*, 2013, Apprentice House/ Loyola University. Forthcoming in 2017 from Main Street Rag, her new collection of poems, *Bistro in Another Realm*. Favorite ice cream flavor: Vanilla in a sugar cone!

Michael Brockley is a 66-year old school psychologist who has worked in special education in rural northeast Indiana for 28 years. Brockley has placed recent work in *Flying Island, Panoplyzine, Third Wednesday* and *Zingara Poetry Picks*. As a child, Brockley's favorite ice cream was strawberry; now he has difficulty narrowing his choices to two flavors. Among those that are often chosen are coconut, butter pecan, black walnut, pistachio, pumpkin, peach and, of course, strawberry.

Nancy Canyon loves Mallard Ice Cream in Bellingham. Current dairy-free flavors include Raspberry Lemon Ice and Coconut Ice. "Blood Orange gelato at Chocolate Decadence sends me." Her earliest memory of ice cream includes sucking rock salt from the churn late one hot summer night then eating bowlfuls of creamy vanilla in the dark. "As a teen," Nancy says, "I made 'ices' from recipes found in *Fanny Farmer Cookbook*." For writing and visual art by Nancy see: www.nancycanyon.com

Neil Carpathios is the author of four poetry collections, *Confessions of a Captured Angel* (Terrapin Books, 2016), *Playground of Flesh* (Main Street Rag), *At the Axis of Imponderables* (Quercus Review Press Book Award), and *Beyond the Bones* (FutureCycle Press), and editor of the anthology *Every River on Earth: Writing from Appalachian Ohio* (Ohio University Press). Now an associate professor of English at Shawnee State University in Portsmouth, Ohio, he fondly remembers his father, who grew up poor in Greece and longed for ice cream as a child, eating it every night after coming to America.

"The One True Word" originally appeared in *At the Axis of Imponderables* (Winner of the Quercus Review Press Book Award, 2007).

Tom Chatburn was born in Germantown, Philadelphia in 1935. His father was drafted into the Second World War at age 33. His favorite and earliest ice cream memory was spent that summer at a camp in Stone Harbor, NJ. His grandparents sent letters with dimes taped inside, and he bought Apricot Sherbet at a stand at the end of the street. Tom had a 25-year career in Advertising with Sears, and with his wife Pat operated two retail stores.

Lucia Cherciu is a Professor of English at SUNY/ Dutchess in Poughkeepsie, NY, and her new book, *Train Ride to Bucharest,* is forthcoming from Sheep Meadow Press. Her other books include *Edible Flowers* (Main Street Rag, 2010), *Lepădarea de Limbă/The Abandonment of Language* (Vinea, 2009), and *Altoiul Râsului/Grafted Laughter* (Brumar 2010). Her poetry was nominated twice for a Pushcart Prize and Best of the Net. Her web page is luciacherciu.webs.com.

Martha Christina has loved ice cream ever since her first childhood visit to relatives who hand-cranked their own. Cones, sundaes, sodas, novelties–all hold her in thrall. Nevertheless, "Easy Enough" is the only poem of hers in which ice cream appears. Short poems on other subjects appear frequently in *Brevities*, and longer work has been published in *Bryant Literary Review, Crab Orchard Review, The Orange Room Review, Red Eft Review*, and elsewhere.

George David Clark is an assistant professor of English at Washington & Jefferson College. His first book, *Reveille* (Arkansas, 2015), won the Miller Williams Prize, and his new work can be found in *AGNI, The Cincinnati Review, The Gettysburg Review, Image*, and elsewhere. He edits the journal *32 Poems* and lives with his wife and their three young children in Washington, PA. His favorite ice cream is orange sherbet.

"Reveille with Kazoo" first appeared in *Quarterly West 67* (2009) and was published in book form in *Reveille* (Arkansas, 2015).

Joanne M. Clarkson's fourth poetry collection, *Believing the Body*, was published in 2014 by Gribble Press. She was awarded a 2014 GAP grant from Artist Trust to complete her next full-length volume about Fate. Poems have appeared recently in *Rhino, The Baltimore Review, The Healing Muse* and *Fjords Review*. Her favorite ice cream flavor is Spumoni, and one of her best childhood memories is helping cousins hand-crank the homemade strawberry-vanilla variety!

Gail Braune Comorat is a founding member of Rehoboth Beach Writers' Guild. She's the author of *Phases of the Moon* (Finishing Line Press), and has been published in *Grist, Adanna, Gargoyle, Mudfish*, and *The Widows' Handbook*. She received a 2011 Delaware Division of the Arts Fellowship Grant for Emerging

Poet, and a 2015 grant for Established Poet. She loves eating her favorite Ben & Jerry's Americone Dream straight from its pint container.

Chella Courington is the author of three poetry and three flash fiction chapbooks. Her poetry and stories appear in numerous anthologies and journals including *SmokeLong Quarterly*, *Nano Fiction*, and *The Collagist*. Her recent novella, *The Somewhat Sad Tale of the Pitcher and the Crow*, is available at Amazon. Her favorite ice cream is homemade vanilla and favorite ice cream parlor is McConnell's.

"Mama's Orchid" was first published under the title "Georgia O 'Keeffe: Pastel, 1941" in *Phoebe 19.2* (Fall 2007).

Jackie Craven traveled the Rocky Road toward publication. While consuming unhealthy amounts of that flavor, she began as a journalist but now writes poetry for places like *New Ohio Review, Nimrod, Salamander*, and *Water~Stone Review*. Her chapbook, *Our Lives Became Unmanageable*, won the Omnidawn Fabulist Fiction Award. Jackie enjoys the nuttiest ice cream in upstate New York and the chocolaty-est in Cocoa Beach, Florida. Visit her at www.JackieCraven.com.

"Postcards I Wish I'd Sent Lisbeth When We Were Girls and Her Parents Sent Her Away" was first published in *The Fourth River* in 2014.

Barbara Crooker is the author of six books of poetry; *Barbara Crooker: Selected Poems* is the most recent. She has received a number of awards, including the 2004 WB Yeats Society of New York Award, the 2003 Thomas Merton Poetry of the Sacred Award, and three

Pennsylvania Council on the Arts Creative Writing Fellowships. Her work has been read many times on *The Writer's Almanac*, and her favorite ice cream is Chocolat Noir, from Berthillon, Ile Saint-Louis, Paris.

"*L 'Atelier Rose*, 1911" was first published in *Nimrod*, 2012. "Sugar" was first published in *Poet Lore*, then in the poet's collection *Gold* (Cascade Books, 2013).

Dana Beardsley Crotwell teaches poetry, literature, and composition at El Camino College in Torrance, California. She has published poems in a variety of anthologies, journals, and magazines. She enjoys eating ice cream with her family and friends. She feels Baskin Robbins Quarterback Crunch is her favorite football memory. Her store-bought flavor of choice used to be Tiramisu before her husband Kevin unearthed the conspiracy surrounding its disappearance.

John Davis is the author of *Gigs* and *The Reservist*. He teaches writing, performs in rock and roll bands, and lives on an island near Seattle. He is enamored with cinnamon ice cream which he eats slowly but deliberately to fight off ice cream headaches. Among his early memories are hand-cranking vanilla and root beer ice cream with his father.

Daniel de Cullá is a writer, poet, and photographer. He is also a member of the Spanish Writers Association, Earthly Writers International Caucus, Poets of the World, and others. He is the Director of *Gallo Tricolor Review* and *Robespierre Review*. He has participated in Festivals of Poetry, and Theater in Madrid, Burgos, Berlin, Minden, Hannover and Genève. His favorite ice cream is mint chocolate chip.

"Holy, Holy" first appeared in *In Between Hangovers* (October 2016).

Lori Desrosiers' books are *The Philosopher's Daughter* (Salmon Poetry 2013), a chapbook, *Inner Sky* (Glass Lyre Press, 2015) and *Sometimes I Hear the Clock Speak* (Salmon Poetry, 2016). She edits *Naugatuck River Review*, a journal of narrative poetry, and *WORDPEACE*, an online journal dedicated to peace and justice. Her work has appeared in numerous journals, and she has been nominated for a Pushcart Prize. Her favorite ice cream flavors are coffee, chocolate, and almond anything.

Deborah H. Doolittle has lived in lots of different places but now calls North Carolina home. She teaches at Coastal Carolina Community College. Some of her work has recently appeared or will soon appear in *Pinyon, Poetalk,* and *Shemom*. Her first collection of poems, *Floribunda*, was released spring 2017 from Main Street Rag. Sitting up at the counter at Lincoln Dairy and eating watermelon ice cream was a special childhood treat.

Karl Elder is Lakeland University's Fessler Professor of Creative Writing and Poet in Residence. *Gilgamesh at the Bellagio*, from National Poetry Review Press, is his ninth collection of poetry. Among his honors are the Christopher Latham Sholes Award from the Council for Wisconsin Writers and a Pushcart Prize. Elder's recent novel, *Earth as It Is in Heaven*, is from Pebblebrook Press; he imagines the main character would prefer peppermint of all flavors of ice cream.

Kristina England resides in Worcester, Massachusetts. She is a writer and photographer. Her writing has been published in several magazines, including *New*

Verse News, Silver Birch Press, Tipton Poetry Journal, and *Topology.* She can be followed at https://www.facebook.com/kristinadengland. Ms. England's favorite type of ice cream is chocolate peanut butter chunk in any brand. She often has a freezer chock full of tubs to ensure she doesn't run low on her vital dessert.

Susan J. Erickson chooses coffee, both in ice cream cone and cup. Susan lives in Bellingham, Washington, where she helped establish the Sue C. Boynton Poetry Walk and Contest. She has completed a manuscript of poems in women's voices. Those poems appear in *Raven's Chronicles, 2River View, Crab Creek Review, James Franco Review, Museum of Americana, The Fourth River, Naugatuck River Review, Literal Latte* and others.

Michael Estabrook is retired. No more useless meetings under florescent lights in stuffy windowless rooms, able instead to focus on making better poems when he's not, of course, endeavoring to satisfy his wife's legendary Honey-Do List. His latest collection of poems is *Bouncy House*, edited by Larry Fagin (Green Zone Editions, 2016). Vanilla, believe it or not, is his favorite ice cream He worked at a Carvel's Ice Cream Stand through high school back in the 1960s, best job he ever had!

Jeanne Ferran is a teacher. Although she grew up in New Orleans, she currently calls the mountains of western North Carolina home. She regularly bribes her two preschool-aged sons with ice cream (chocolate) if they receive gold stars on their daily folders. Her favorite ice cream memory is going to Marina Grill in New Orleans with her family to feast on Nectar Sodas and Coke Floats after graduations and performances.

Alice B. Fogel is New Hampshire's poet laureate. Her 2015 collection, *Interval: Poems Based on Bach's "Goldberg Variations,"* won the Nicholas Schaffner Award for Music in Literature. *Be That Empty* was a national bestseller, and she is also the author of the guide for readers and teachers, *Strange Terrain*, on how to appreciate poetry without "getting" it. Her town's cows, more numerous than humans, provide Walpole Creamery Ice Cream; her favorites are coconut and ginger.

Laura Foley is the author of six poetry collections, including, most recently, *WTF* and *Night Ringing*. Her poem "Gratitude List" won the Common Good Books poetry contest and was read by Garrison Keillor on *The Writer's Almanac*. Her poem "Nine Ways of Looking at Light" won the Joe Gouveia Outermost Poetry Contest, judged by Marge Piercy. Her favorite ice cream is coffee, sprinkled with malted milk. She remembers eating this at the beach, as a child, on Fisher's Island. The texture and color of malt was just like sand, and yet how wonderfully sweet.

"Gelato" appeared in *Joy Street* (Headmistress Press).

"The Happy Apartment" appeared in *Night Ringing* (Headmistress Press).

Debra M. Fox is the director of an adoption agency. She is the published author of haiku, short stories, and essays. She lives on the outskirts of Philadelphia with her husband, younger son who is profoundly disabled, and a companion dog who aspired to be a service dog but failed. When she was pregnant, she craved mint chocolate chip ice cream. Her dutiful husband saw that she was well supplied. Visit her online at debramfox.com.

Claudia Gary eats less ice cream and enjoys it more than during her "Ballet Routine" years. Author of *Humor Me* (David Robert Books, 2006), she is a three-time Howard Nemerov Sonnet Award finalist. Claudia's poems appear in journals internationally; her health articles appear in *The VVA Veteran* and elsewhere. Her recent chapbooks, *Bikini Buyer's Remorse* and *Let's Get Out of Here*, are available via the email address in pw.org/content/claudia_gary.

"Ballet Routine" was originally published in *The Rotary Dial* (Canada).

Monique Gordon lives in Philadelphia, PA with Endo Jesús Paws and Freya Staticē Sage, her two rescue pets. These treasured souls act as muses for offbeat poetry, as well as a reminder for her to test her blood sugar. Arctic Zero Vanilla Maple is her favorite frozen dessert. Her earliest ice-cream memory is having Russell The Yum-Yum Man triple dipping and muddying vats to make a rainbow. You can find Monique blogging about living with Type 1 Diabetes (tips, quirks, and laughs) @ www.moniquegordon.wordpress.com

Aimee Harris lives in North Jersey where she works as a librarian and recently facilitated a program about ice cream including how to make it using just ice, salt, plastic bags, and a few simple ingredients. She enjoys making it for her husband and son at home in her ice cream maker; one of her favorite flavor combinations so far is white chocolate cinnamon cherry. She has a MFA in Creative Writing from Emerson College.

"The War Was Won With Ice Cream" appeared in the December 21, 2013 issue of *Referential Magazine*.

Faleeha Hassan, a poet, teacher, editor, and writer born in Najaf, Iraq, is the first woman to write poetry for children in Iraq. She leads a poetic feminist movement in the holy city of Najaf. She received a master's degree in Arabic literature, and published twenty poetry collections in Arabic and English. Her poems have been translated into French, Italian, German, Kurdish, Spanish, and many other languages. She loves the ice cream in Turkey, made fresh in front of the customer with the flavor she loves.

"Two Doves" appears in previous versions online in at Iamnotasilentpoet.wordpress.com, HelloPoetry.com, and NonDoc.com

Margaret Hasse lives in Saint Paul, Minnesota, where she's active in the poetry community as a writer, teacher, and activist. Author of five collections of poems, her latest is *Between Us*. She's received a National Endowment for the Arts poetry fellowship, among other honors. When she first read Steven's "The Emperor of Ice-Cream," she didn't understand it referred to serving ice cream at a funeral, but she was drawn by the poem's words and sounds.

"Snow Ice Cream" appears in Margaret Hasse's poetry collection *Between Us* (Nodin Press, 2016).

Grey Held is a recipient of a National Endowment for the Arts Fellowship in Creative Writing. Two books of his poems have been published: *Two-Star General* was published by Brick Road Poetry Press in 2012 and *Spilled Milk* was published by Word Press in 2013. In his home town of Newton, MA, he directs projects that connect contemporary poets with a wider audience. When it comes to frozen flavors, it's butter rum undoes his tongue.

Esther Altshul Helfgott is the author of *Listening to Mozart: Poems of Alzheimer's* (Yakima, WA: Cave Moon Press, 2014), *Dear Alzheimer's: A Caregiver's Diary & Poems* (Yakima, WA: Cave Moon Press, 2013) and *The Homeless One: A Poem in Many Voices* (Seattle: Kota Press, 2000), among other works. She loves pistachio ice cream and still waits for the Good Humor Man's truck to come down her street with chocolate-covered vanilla Good Humor bars. Yum.

"I Dream of Uncle Benny and Strawberries" has been published in *DRASH:* Northwest Mosaic, 2009, and as part of an essay "Edith Buxbaum, Latency and Me - Between the Oedipus Complex and Adolescence: The Quiet Time - Letter to Edith," *Journal of Poetry Therapy*, Volume 19, Number 2, June 2006, pp. 83-90.

Elissa Hoffman adores ice cream and her favorite flavor is coffee. She rates dill pickle worst. Steve's Ice Cream was her dream ice cream parlor. A child psychiatrist, she earned an MD from Albert Einstein College of Medicine, an MFA in creative nonfiction at West Virginia University, and a BA in English literature from Princeton University. Her essay "Cutting Time" appeared in *Kestrel*. She has had poems published in *Voices from the Attic*.

Rebe Huntman's essays and poems appear in *Ninth Letter, Sonora Review, South Loop Review, The Pinch, Tampa Review, Quarter After Eight*, and elsewhere. A former professional Latin dancer, she holds an MFA in creative nonfiction from The Ohio State University and teaches creative writing at the Columbus College of Art and Design. Her favorite ice cream memory is mixing Hershey's syrup into vanilla ice cream. Find her at www.rebehuntman.com.

"Mother with Paul Newman and Small Axis" was first published in *Ninth Letter*, Spring 2016.

Scott T. Hutchison's work has appeared in *The Georgia Review* and *The Southern Review*. As if ice cream weren't wonderful enough—add in first love, and life becomes a treat.

Wendy Elizabeth Ingersoll is a retired piano teacher who at age 68 likes to treat herself with a dish of sherbet, especially orange. Her book *Grace Only Follows* won the National Federation of Press Women Contest. She's been published in *Naugatuck River Review, Connecticut River Review, Passager, Gargoyle, Mojave River Review, Delmarva Review, Broadkill Review*, and *Worcester Review*. Her manuscript *White Crane Spreads Its Wings* was a Finalist for the Dogfish Head Poetry Prize in 2015.

Gerda Govine Ituarte has published three books of poetry, *Future Awakes in Mouth of NOW, Oh, Where is My Candle Hat?* and *Alterations|Thread Light Through Eye of Storm*, in English and Spanish. Her poems appeared in journals, online, art exhibits, and newspapers. She has read her work in Canada, Colombia, Cuba, London, Mexico, and the US. Her mother worked in an ice cream parlor and every day after school, she and her brother stopped in for ice cream treats of their choosing: plain, malted, ice cream soda or egg creme. She was in heaven.

"Poster Boy" was included in *Dryland Literature Los Angeles Underground Art & Writing Anthology*, Summer 2015 and *Coiled Serpent Anthology: Poems Arising from the Cultural Quakes & Shifts of Los Angeles* (Tia Chucha Press, 2016).

Jill McCabe Johnson is the author of two books of poetry, *Diary of the One Swelling Sea* (MoonPath Press, 2013), winner of a Nautilus Book Award, and *Revolutions We'd Hoped We'd Outgrown* (Finishing Line, 2017). Given the chance, she would eat ice cream for every meal. Now she can read it instead. (Or better yet, eat ice cream while reading it!)

"North Beach, Low Tide" was first published in *Revolutions We'd Hoped We'd Outgrown* (Finishing Line, 2017).

Bonnie S. Kaplan is a native Angeleno and a longtime teacher of adults in the California corrections system. A 2015 Pushcart nominee, her poems are published in *Adrienne Rich: A Tribute Anthology, This Assignment is So Gay: LGBTIQ Poets on the Art of Teaching,*82 Review 2.2, Out of Sequence: The Sonnets Remixed* and online in *Cultural Weekly*. Rocky Road was a favorite childhood ice cream flavor because of its complexity.

Ruth Moon Kempher was in her thirties when she and her artist husband J moved to St. Augustine, Florida in 1960. Years later, she's taught college students and written poems and gotten lots older and owned a tavern and drank and always scotch and had wonderful dogs and never ate any ice cream that wasn't chocolate. Last November she rescued a wonderful sweet lady dog, and Brie's a chocolate lab of course. This February, Chiron Review Press published Ruth's book *The Skinny about J's Zinnias*, with J's Zinnias on the cover: Life is Good.

"Baked Red Mullet" was first published in *Minotaur*, ed. Jim Watson-Gove, 2013.

Diane Kendig's fifth poetry collection, *Prison Terms*, was a finalist for the Cathy Smith Bowers contest. When she was little, her maternal grandfather told her his story of the excitement when the first cones came to his childhood hometown around 1910. After eating the ice cream, he returned with his empty cone, saying, "That's good! Can I have another?" Any flavor on a sugar cone remains her favorite way to indulge. She blogs at dianekendig.blogspot.com.

Maria Blanchard's "*El carrito del helado* (The Ice Cream Cart)" was first published in *Ekphrasis*.

Hunter Keough is an undergraduate student at the University of Memphis. He is expected to graduate in December 2016 with a degree in Creative Writing, at which point he intends to pursue an MFA in Poetry. Hunter is also a recurring poet in the *Tennessee Magazine*. His favorite ice cream flavor is mint chocolate chip.

Patty Kinney is a Pushcart nominee whose work has appeared in *The Sun, Crab Creek Review, Floating Bridge Review, Human Journal, Examined Life Journal,* and other places. She embraces the moon and remembers graduating from baby spoon to big people's spoon to eat vanilla ice cream on her 2nd birthday. Patty holds an MFA in nonfiction and poetry, and recently completed a full-length collection, *Fertility Is A Found Object*. She fed her six sons ice cream—often.

Janet R. Kirchheimer is the author of "How to Spot One of Us." She is producing *AFTER*, a cinematic film showcasing poetry about the Holocaust. Her work appears in many journals and online including *Belmont Story Review, Limestone, Connecticut Review, Lilith, Natural Bridge* and *Bearings Online*. She is a Pushcart Prize nominee who, every summer, promised to clean her room while begging her mother for money so she could buy a Chocolate Eclair from the Good Humor man.

Kaaren Kitchell, a writer who lives in Paris, has had poems published in literary journals and anthologies, and in her book, *The Minotaur Dance*. She received an MFA in Creative Writing from Antioch University, LA, and has completed a novel, *The Book of Twelve*, about the revolutionary 1960s. Since 2011, she and Richard Beban have published her essays and his photos in *Paris Play*: www.parisplay.com. She is Fiction Editor and Co-Poetry Editor of *TheScreamOnline*.

Linda Lancione writes poetry, personal essays, and fiction and has co-authored two travel books. Her work has appeared widely in literary journals such as *Cimarron Review, CrazyHorse, New Letters, Notre Dame Review, Post Road*, and *Southern Indiana Review* as well as in four poetry chapbooks. In 2010, she won the New Letters Prize for Best Essay; other awards include residency fellowships at the Helene Wurlitzer Foundation and Montalvo Center for the Arts. A former teacher of English as a Second Language, she lives in the San Francisco Bay Area. Favorite flavors: coffee, blood orange.

"Note to Mom" first appeared in Linda's chapbook of related poems, *The Taste of Blood*, (Finishing Line Press, 2016).

Joan Leotta has been playing with words since her Pittsburgh childhood. She fell in love with the creaminess of vanilla ice cream at her father's drugstore. She loves lemon Italian ice and has sampled pistachio gelato all over Italy. She now lives in Calabash, NC where she walks the beach, eating ice cream, with husband Joe. She has six books in print, poems in many journals and is an onstage story performer. www.joanleotta.wordpress.com and https://www.facebook.com/pages/Joan-Leotta-Author-and-Story-Performer/188479350973

Carol Levin's publications include two full volumes of poetry, *Confident Music Would Fly Us to Paradise* and *Stunned By the Velocity*, and the chapbooks, *Red Rooms and Others* and *Sea Lions Sing Scat*. She's an Editorial Assistant at *Crab Creek Review* and teaches The Breathing Lab/Alexander Technique in Seattle. The plea, in the poem "Bury Me," was fervently meant to plead for Dryers Ice Cream to market *mint with candies*. They ignored her desperation.

John Manesis is a retired physician whose poetry has been published in over 90 literary publications. He has four full length poetry books to his credit, all available at amazon.com: *With All My Breath, Other Candle Lights, Consider, If You Will*, and *In the Third Season*. He comes from a family of restaurateurs and on many occasions provided customers with ice cream and sampled many of his creations along the way. Strawberry is his favorite flavor.

"City Park Sundries" appeared in *With All My Breath* in 2003.

Shahé Mankerian's manuscript, *History of Forgetfulness*, has been a finalist at four prestigious competitions: the 2013 Crab Orchard Series in Poetry Open Competition, the 2013

Bibby First Book Competition, the Quercus Review Press, Fall Poetry Book Award (2013), and the 2014 White Pine Press Poetry Prize. As a child, Shahé remembers tasting boysenberry ice cream in Lebanon at Patisserie Charbel. No ice cream parlor in America has been able to recreate that initial Mediterranean taste.

"Defining Divorce at Five" appeared in *Puff Puff Prose, Poetry and a Play*, Volume III, Edition 2 / 2015.

Fran Markover lives in Ithaca, NY where she writes poems published in journals including *Rattle, Calyx, Runes, Spillway*, and *Karamu*. She is a Pushcart Prize nominee and has a chapbook, *History's Trail*, published by Finishing Line Press. She's also a lover of bittersweet ice cream from Good Humor farm days as a little girl to her favorite ice cream parlors as sweet-craving adult: Purity Ice Cream Parlor and Cayuga Lake Creamery.

Joan Mazza has worked as a medical microbiologist, psychotherapist, and seminar leader, and has been a Pushcart Prize and Best of the Net nominee. Author of six self-help psychology books, including *Dreaming Your Real Self*, her poetry has appeared in *Rattle, Kestrel, The MacGuffin, Mezzo Cammin*, and *The Nation*. She ran away from the hurricanes of South Florida to be surprised by the earthquakes and tornadoes of rural Virginia, where she writes poetry and does paper art. www.JoanMazza.com

Tamara MC is an Applied Linguist who focuses on issues related to language, culture, and identity in the Middle East and beyond. Specifically, she writes and researches her hybrid identity of growing up simultaneously Jewish and Muslim. One of her first memories of ice cream is going to Baskin Robbins with her mother and their Weimaraner, Tasha. Tamara ordered gumball ice cream, her mom ordered Pralines and Cream, and they always ordered Tasha "doggie" ice cream.

Kathleen McClung, author of *Almost the Rowboat*, has poems in *Mezzo Cammin, Unsplendid, Atlanta Review, Ekphrasis, West Trestle Review, Raising Lilly Ledbetter: Women Poets Occupy the Workspace*, and elsewhere. Winner of the Rita Dove Poetry Prize, McClung judges sonnets for the Soul-Making Keats literary competition. She teaches at Skyline College and the Writing Salon and lives in San Francisco. She earned her first paycheck at 17 scooping ice cream and looking out the window. www.kathleenmcclung.com.

"Instructions for Closing" was published online in *Mezzo Cammin*, Volume 11, Issue 2.

Michael Meyerhofer is the author of four books of poetry, as well as a fantasy series. For more info, visit troublewithhammers.com. In the meantime, his favorite ice cream is anything that involves peanut butter, but no nuts and/or random chunks of fruit, because that's just wrong. He's also partial to Butterfinger ice cream, especially when it melts, thus opening a gateway into Nirvana.

Penelope Moffet's first memories of ice cream (actually, ice milk) are from those exciting and rare early-childhood nights when Dad would come home with the treat and wake up all the kids to share it. Much later, real ice cream was a revelation. Moffet has published poems in various magazines, including *The*

Missouri Review, Columbia, The Broome Review, Permafrost, Pearl, Steam Ticket, The MacGuffin, and *Riverwind.*

Alice Morris, a Minnesota native, has poems in *The Broadkill Review, The White Space,* and *A Collection of Dance Poems,* and work forthcoming in anthologies and a love-themed collection. She comes to writing with a background in art, published in *The New York Art Review.* Fondly, she recalls riding a golf cart around Smith Island (vehicles banned) with husband and daughter, stopping each evening at the island's only ice cream shop. Choosing vanilla, blackberry, raspberry, or pistachio?

Erika Mueller is a poet, mother, and former ice cream parlor employee. She enjoys eating spoonfuls of Mint Galactica Coconut Bliss while reading poems as an assistant editor of *Cream City Review.* She holds an MFA from the University of Oregon and a PhD in Creative Writing from the University of WI-Milwaukee. Her poems have recently appeared in *Crab Orchard Review, Duende,* and elsewhere.

Sharon Lask Munson is a poet, retired teacher, coffee junkie, wine devotee, old movie enthusiast, and lover of chocolate ice cream. She grew up in Detroit, Michigan; every evening in the summer she would get her single dip from Haney's Ice Cream and Candy Shop. She is the author of *Stillness Settles Down the Lane, That Certain Blue,* and *Braiding Lives.* She lives and writes in Eugene, Oregon.

Bruce W. Niedt is a retired civil servant whose poetry has appeared in numerous publications, including

Writers Digest, Rattle, Spitball, The Lyric, US 1 Worksheets,
and the anthologies *Best of The Barefoot Muse* and *Poem Your Heart Out.* He has been nominated twice for the Pushcart Prize. His latest chapbook is *Hits and Sacrifices,* published by Finishing Line Press. He lives about a mile from the best frozen custard stand in South Jersey.

"Mercurochrome Summer" was previously published in *Chantarelle's Notebook,* December 2012.

Nancy Pagh is the author of *Write Moves: A Creative Writing Guide & Anthology* and three collections of poetry, most recently *Once Removed* from MoonPath Press. Her work appears in numerous journals, including *Prairie Schooner, Canadian Literature, Crab Creek Review, Bellingham Review, Valparaiso Poetry Review, RHINO, Poetry Northwest, Rattle,* and *O* magazine. She teaches at Western Washington University. Although partial to chocolate, her current favorite ice cream is cardamom at Mallard's Ice Cream in Bellingham.

Vincent Peloso is a one-time finalist for the "Discovery"/Nation award, a past participant in the Squaw Valley Community of Writers, and first runner-up for the 2011 Bordighera Poetry Prize. He lives in Fortuna, CA with his wife and dog, all of whom love ice cream and often find themselves thinking, "Well, if we buy the low-fat option, we can eat twice as much, right?"

"Where Are You Now, Elizabeth Doss" was previously published in the *Noyo River Review,* Summer 2014.

Meg J. Petersen is the director of the National Writing Project in New Hampshire at Plymouth State

University, where she teaches courses on writing and the teaching of writing. This past year she was on a Fulbright grant working with a group of teachers in the Dominican Republic to found a writing project site there. Her favorite ice cream flavors reflect these two cultures: maple walnut and coconut/mango.

Wanda S. Praisner, a recipient of fellowships from the NJ State Council on the Arts, Dodge Foundation, Provincetown Fine Arts Center, and VCCA, has won the Egan Award, Princemere Prize, Kudzu Competition, and First Prize in Poetry at the College of NJ Writers' Conference. An eight-time Pushcart nominee, she appears in *Atlanta Review, Lullwater Review,* and *Prairie Schooner.* Her latest book is *Sometimes When Something Is Singing* (Antrim House, 2014). She is a resident poet for the state.

Erin Redfern wrote "Finale" for the San Jose Mission Chamber Orchestra's 2015 Noteworthy Desserts benefit. The poem had to incorporate two subjects: mandarin chocolate ice cream from Marianne's (a Santa Cruz institution since 1947), and the fourth movement of Brahms's Piano Quintet in F Minor, with its contemplative opening, vigorous bridge, and final tug of war between them. www.erinredfern.net

Susan Rich is author of four collections of poems including *Cloud Pharmacy* and *The Alchemist's Kitchen;* she has received awards from the Fulbright Foundation, PEN USA, and the Times Literary Supplement. Rich's work appears in *The Gettysburg Review, New England Review* and *Poetry Ireland.* She teaches at Highline College. As a child, Susan and her father planned to review all of the out-of-the-way ice cream shops throughout New England. Their book was to be called *Quick, Before It Melts!* Her newest career plan is to open an ice cream parlor in Seattle specializing in cardamom affogatos. The "Elevated" in the title refers to Elevated Ice Cream, Port Townsend, WA.

Judith R. Robinson is an editor, teacher, fiction writer and poet. A 1980 summa cum laude graduate of the University of Pittsburgh, she is listed in the *Directory of American Poets and Writers.* She has published 100 plus poems, four poetry collections, one fiction collection and edited or co-edited eleven poetry collections. Teacher: Osher at Carnegie Mellon University, U. of Pittsburgh. Ice cream: Baskin-Robbins Rocky Road; Yummy!

"This Summer Moment" was first published in *Main Street Rag*, Spring, 2016.

"This Summer Moment" was also published in *Carousel*, Lummox Press, 2017.

Susan Roney-O'Brien lives in Princeton, Massachusetts. She is the readings curator for The Thirsty Lab and the summer writing program coordinator for the Stanley Kunitz House. Her poems have appeared in *Prairie Schooner, Concrete Wolf, Beloit Poetry Journal* and many other journals. Two of her chapbooks have been published: *Farmwife* and *Earth.* Word Press published her book, *Legacy of the Last World*, in March of 2016, and she celebrated with ginger ice cream.

M.S. Rooney lives in Sonoma, California with her husband, poet Dan Noreen. Her work appears in journals, including *Bluestem, The Cortland Review, Illuminations,* and *Main Street Rag,* and anthologies, including *American Society: What Poets See,* edited by David Chorlton and Robert S. King. Her work has been nominated for a Pushcart Prize. Growing up in Sacramento, she pursued the art of finishing a Sidewalk Sundae before the ice cream melted off the stick in triple-digit summer weather.

John Rowe is president of the Bay Area Poets Coalition. His most recent poetry chapbook is *Beyond Perspective* (Finishing Line Press, 2015). His North Berkeley, CA hometown neighborhood had two old-fashioned ice cream parlors less than a block apart, plus "31 Flavors" down the street (all only memories now). Rocky Road was a favorite flavor from childhood. He's always enjoyed quality scoops of coffee, strawberry, or vanilla.

Nicholas Samaras won the Yale Series of Younger Poets Award with his first book, *Hands of the Saddlemaker.* His latest book of poetry is *American Psalm, World Psalm* (Ashland Poetry Press, 2014). He is currently completing a new book of poetry and a memoir of his youth lived underground in nine different countries, remembering each country by its quality of ice-cream (Belgium was a great country for ice-cream). Recently returned from the Greek Islands, Nick found the amazing flavor of pomegranate ice-cream, highly recommended.

"Beach Concession Stand on Long Island Sound" was first published in *The New York Times.*

Judith Sanders' poem "Homage" won the 2012 Hart Crane Memorial Poetry Contest sponsored by Kent

State University; another poem, "Shoppin' Spree," won the 2012 Humor Poetry Prize sponsored by WinningWriters.com. Her poems and articles have appeared in anthologies, journals, and the *Pittsburgh Post-Gazette*. She teaches English at Winchester Thurston School in Pittsburgh. Summer to her means a mocha frappe from PJs on Cape Cod.

"The Treat" was first published in the *Pittsburgh Post-Gazette*, October 31, 2009.

Care Santos is the author of over 40 books in different genres, including novels, short story collections, young adult and children's books, and poetry. She has won numerous prizes and awards, including the Primavera Prize, the Ateneo Joven de Sevilla, the Gran Angular prize for young adult literature, and the Barco de Vapor prize for young adult literature, among many others. Two of her books have been translated into English, the novel *Desire for Chocolate* (Alma Books, 2015) and the poetry collection *Dissection* (A Midsummer Night's Press, 2014).

Lawrence Schimel writes in both Spanish and English and has published over 100 books in many different genres as author or anthologist. He has won the Lambda Literary Award (twice), the Spectrum Award, the Independent Publisher Book Award, the Rhysling Award, and other honors. He is also the publisher of A Midsummer Night's Press. He lives in Madrid, Spain, where he works as a Spanish-English translator.

Penelope Scambly Schott has received the Oregon Book Award for Poetry. Her newest books are *Serpent Love: A Mother-Daughter Epic* and *Bailing the River*. She lives in Portland where she hosts the White Dog Poetry Salon and also in Dufur, Oregon where she teaches an annual workshop. Bulletin: Penelope has recently discovered Ruby Jewel honey-lavender ice cream sandwiches with lemon shortbread biscuits, a life-changing experience.

"Perspective" was originally published in *How I Became an Historian* (Cherry Grove, 2014).

Thom Schramm's poems have appeared in many journals, including *The American Scholar*, *New Letters*, *Ploughshares*, and *Poetry Northwest*. He is the editor of *Living in Storms: Contemporary Poetry and the Moods of Manic-Depression* (Eastern Washington University Press, 2008). In 2016, Blue Cubicle Press published his chapbook *The Leaf Blower*. As a child, he enjoyed black licorice ice cream.

"Wake: 1978" originally appeared in *Poet Lore* (Fall/ Winter 2006).

Harvey Schwartz learned Americana growing up on the east coast. He unlearned it at Woodstock, a hippie commune, and during extensive hitchhiking. A long chiropractic career offered another perspective. As an eight-year-old he agonized over a banana split that he couldn't afford. A kindly stranger made up the difference and this bio is his confession that he pocketed the difference and bought a small cone, a decision that he still regrets.

Nancy Scott, managing editor of *U.S.1 Worksheets* based in New Jersey, is the author of nine collections of poetry; her most recent, *Ah, Men* (Aldrich Press, 2016), is a retrospective on the men who influenced her life. The creamiest ice cream came in a cone from Griffiths Dairy, but nothing was better than sharing a banana split at the soda fountain with Danny or slurping a rootbeer float at the Carousel Drive-in. www.nancyscott.net

"The Good Humor Man, 1960" was first published in the author's book, *Down to the Quick* (Plain View Press, 2007).

Heidi Seaborn is known to bike 20 miles, take a ferry and a water taxi for her favorite Mora blackberry ice cream. Living in Seattle, Heidi started writing poetry in 2016. Since then, her work has appeared in over 20 journals including *Gravel, West Trade Review, Into the Void, Vine Leaves Literary Journal, Gold Man Review,* and *Carbon Culture Review,* in five anthologies, as the chapbook *Body Politic* published by Mount Analogue Press, and on a Seattle bus. www.heidiseabornpoet.com

Tim Sherry, a longtime public school teacher and administrator, lives in Tacoma, Washington. His poems have appeared in *Rattle, Raven Chronicles, Broad River Review, Windfall,* and others. He has been a Pushcart nominee and Artsmith Artist Resident, and had work recognized in competitions. His first full-length collection, *One of Seven Billion,* was published by MoonPath Press in 2014. His best ice cream memory is vanilla with coffee one night in Paris long ago when all the stars were out.

Shoshauna Shy's poetry has recently been published courtesy of *IthacaLit, Carbon Culture Review, RHINO,* and *Sliver of Stone.* She has flash fiction in the public arena or slated to appear thanks to *100 Word Story, Fiction Southeast, Literary Orphans* and *Prairie Wolf Press Review.* On any given day, grasshopper sundaes at the Hubbard Street Diner featuring brownie wedges drowned in hot fudge sauce is choice #1. Ben & Jerry's Half-Baked = Plan B.

Karen Skolfield's book *Frost in the Low Areas (Zone 3)* won the 2014 PEN New England Award in poetry. Her recent fellowships and awards are from the Poetry Society of America, New England Public Radio, Massachusetts Cultural Council, Ucross Foundation, Split This Rock, Hedgebrook, and Vermont Studio Center. She's grateful to live near the farming community of Hadley, Massachusetts, where a local creamery churns out asparagus ice cream every spring.

San Diego artist and musician **Anitra Carol Smith** has published her poetry, nonfiction and photography in print and online and has written two commissioned biographies. With a B.A. in English from Occidental College and an M.A. in literature from UCSD, she is currently finishing the screenplay for her film, "Silent Sparrow," which is expected in summer 2018 from Atlanta's KaeCole Productions. Any good wishes and monetary enthusiasm would be deeply appreciated at the website silentsparrowmovie.com. Anitra considers Baskin Robbins a kind of ashram.

Laurie Stone is the author most recently of *My Life as an Animal*, a book of linked stories. Her work has appeared in *Fence, Open City, Creative Nonfiction, Anderbo*, and many other journals. To learn more about her writing and workshops visit lauriestonewriter.com.

Patrick Swaney's favorite ice cream cone is a chocolate vanilla twist, which sounds boring but is delicious and seems increasingly difficult to find at ice cream shops. On a recent summer evening, he had a perfect chocolate vanilla twist at Fran's Dairy Bar in Millville, Pennsylvania. Patrick lives in Athens, Ohio. He recently completed his Ph.D. in creative writing at Ohio University.

Michael Sweeney is an engineer, writer, and musician living in New York City. He writes creative nonfiction and poetry. His first published essay, entitled "Flood Myth (Or, 'Along the Perimeter')" was featured in *Mount Hope Magazine's* Spring 2016 issue. He believes that ice cream is generally better than gelato, and that, at least when it comes to frozen desserts, it's best to include something savory (like salted nuts or pretzels) to offset the sweetness.

Wally Swist's books include *Huang Po and the Dimensions of Love* (Southern Illinois University Press, 2012); *The Daodejing: A New Interpretation*, with David Breeden and Steven Schroeder (Lamar University Literary Press, 2015); and *Invocation* (Lamar University Literary Press, 2015.) His favorite ice cream is the black raspberry that Flavors of Hadley, Massachusetts makes, and he finds it a particular treat to order two scoops in a cup, especially after hiking on a summer day.

"Upon Request" previously appeared in *Huang Po and the Dimensions of Love* (Southern Illinois University Press, 2012).

Mary Ellen Talley has recently had poems published in *Typoetic.us* and *Kaleidoscope*, as well as in recent anthologies: *All We Can Hold* poems of motherhood,

Raising Lilly Ledbetter Women Poets Occupy the Workspace, and *The Doll Collection*. For her, every summer must include blueberry picking north of Seattle at Bryant's Farm with a stop at Foster's Produce in Arlington, Washington for a cake cone filled with chocolate peanut butter ice cream.

Marilyn L. Taylor, card-carrying ice cream addict who currently favors mint chocolate chip, is the former Poet Laureate of Wisconsin (2009–2010) and author of six poetry collections. Her award-winning work has appeared in many anthologies and journals, including *Poetry, American Scholar, Able Muse*, and *Measure*. She also served for five years as a regular poetry columnist for *The Writer* magazine. She lives in Madison, Wisconsin, where she continues to write and teach.

"Reverie in Sapphics, with Fries" was originally published in *Poemeleon*.

"A Highly Caloric Lament" was originally published in *Passager*.

Molly Tenenbaum is the author of four poetry books, *By a Thread, Now, The Cupboard Artist*, and *Mytheria*; and of *Exercises to Free the Tongue*, an artist book/chapbook collaboration with Ellen Ziegler. Her favorite ice cream is really gelato—from Fainting Goat in Seattle, or Eataly in New York. Her earliest and saddest ice cream memory is of dropping a whole pink grapefruit sherbet on the sidewalk outside of the 31 Flavors.

"I Live in a Yellow Ice-Cream Truck" was previously published in *Now* (Bear Star Press, 2007).

Jeanne Thomas, as a child, liked getting popsicles from the ice cream man. Her all-time favorite ice cream is butter pecan, but she enjoyed lemon custard ice cream during summer visits to Michigan. During a trip to Winter Park, FL, she had a sundae at the Yum Yum Shoppe. She likes Dairy Queen's pineapple milkshakes. Although lemon ice cream is hard to find, she thinks that Haagen-Dazs pineapple coconut ice cream is a delightful treat!

Z.G. Tomaszewski, born in 1989 in Grand Rapids, Michigan, has two books of poems, *All Things Dusk* (International Poetry Prize winner selected by Li-Young Lee and published by Hong Kong University Press, 2015) and the chapbook *Mineral Whisper* (Finishing Line Press, 2017). When eating ice cream he drinks enough water to fill a trough for horses.

Rodney Torreson served as the poet laureate of Grand Rapids, Michigan from 2007-2010. He is the author of four books, his most recent being *The Secrets of Fieldwork*, a chapbook of poems published by Finishing Line Press. His two full-length books are *A Breathable Light* (New Issues Press) and *The Ripening of Pinstripes: Called Shots on the New York Yankees* (Story Line Press).

Julia Park Tracey is the Poet Laureate Emeritus of Alameda, California. She has written essays for *Salon, Redbook, Narratively*, and *Paste*, and has been editor of several print and online magazines. She is an alumnus of the Squaw Valley Community of Writers and lives in Forestville, California. Twitter/Facebook/IG @ juliaparktracey. Favorite ice cream? It's got to be coffee. Two necessities in one scoop.

Linda Tuthill comes from food-crazy Pennsylvania German stock. Her mother occasionally put a wax paper wrapped nickel in her lunchbox for a cone of Breyer's banana at Austy's Grocery Store. Heaven! She frequently writes about the rural world of childhood, but lives in Cleveland. She has been published in *The Auroean* and in Pudding House and Kattywompus Press anthologies. She facilitates poetry classes for Case Western Reserve University's Lifelong Learning Program.

Tim Vincent teaches writing and literature at Duquesne University, Pittsburgh, Pennsylvania. His favorite ice cream parlor is Mary Coyle's, in the Highland Square neighborhood of Akron, Ohio, where he grew up. On summer afternoons, the sidewalk in front of Coyle's would be a tangled heap of bicycles of all sizes and descriptions. In its heyday, Coyle's was one of the happiest places on earth.

Julene Tripp Weaver's current favorite flavor is Nocino, made from black walnuts. It is dense and buttery with a bitter aftertaste. She fondly remembers a summer of daily drives to an east coast Carvel stand for strawberry malteds. Julene is widely published in journals and anthologies. She has three poetry books, just published is *truth be bold—Serenading Life & Death in the Age of AIDS*. Find more at www.julenetrippweaver.com or @trippweavepoet on Twitter.

Michael Dylan Welch loves pralines and cream, or vanilla with orange soda. His life was once saved by ice cream, but that story's too long to fit here. Michael's poems have been recited for the Empress of Japan and at the Baseball Hall of Fame. One of his Japanese translations appeared on 150,000,000 U.S. postage stamps, and he was keynote speaker for the Haiku International Association's 2013 convention in Tokyo. Michael's website is graceguts.com.

"we walk the boardwalk hand in hand" appeared in *Modern Haiku 35:1*, Winter–Spring 2004.

Philip Wexler lives in Bethesda, Maryland, where he also works for the federal government. He has had over 140 of his poems published in magazines over the years and organized a variety of spoken word and music series in the Washington, DC area. He is also a mosaic artist. Although an unabashed fan of good old ice cream, his salivation meter registers higher at the prospect of gelato and sorbet, particularly fruit flavors.

Rhonda Browning White had her first meltdown over ice cream at age five, when a sign at Morgan's Drive Inn read *NOTICE*. She read it as *NOT ICE* and, believing they were out of frozen custard, threw a headline-worthy hissy fit. Since then, she gets ice cream whenever she wants it. You 'll find links to Rhonda's work at www. RhondaBrowningWhite.com. She has an MFA in Creative Writing from Converse College in Spartanburg, SC.

Steve Wilson's poems have appeared in anthologies and journals nationwide, as well as in three books–the most recent of which is entitled *The Lost Seventh*. He teaches in the MFA program at Texas State University. A recent heat wave in Ireland, where he spends his summers, led to the creation of brown bread ice cream at a local restaurant.

Joaquín Zihuatanejo is a poet, World Poetry Slam Champion, and award-winning teacher. An MFA student at the Institute of American Indian Arts, Joaquin's favorite ice cream is Mexican Vanilla with peanut butter cups crushed into it as found at Amy's Ice Cream where he was once the company's youngest assistant manager. Joaquín has two passions in his life, his wife Aída, and poetry, always in that order. Ice cream is a close third.

Ali Znaidi lives in Redeyef, Tunisia. He is the author of several chapbooks, the latest of which is *Mathemaku x5* (Spacecraft Press, 2015). He has a craving for fruit-flavored ice creams, especially strawberry. He also likes chocolate ice cream—a delectable treat, especially while or after writing. For more, visit aliznaidi.blogspot.com.

EDITOR BIOGRAPHY

Patricia Fargnoli, from Walpole NH, was the New Hampshire Poet Laureate from 2006-2009. She's published 5 books and 3 chapbooks of poetry and has won The May Swenson Book Award, the Foreword Magazine Silver Book of the Year Award, the NH Literary Award for Poetry, and the Sheila Mooton Book Award. Her latest book is *Hallowed* (Tupelo Press, 2017). She's published over 300 poems in literary journals such as *Poetry, Ploughshares, Massachusetts Review, Harvard Review* et. al. A Macdowell Fellow and retired social worker, she now teaches poetry privately. You can visit Patricia Fargnoli online at http://www.PatriciaFargnoli.com

She writes: My best memories of ice cream are when the aunt who raised me made it in the hand-cranked ice cream maker with heavy cream and vanilla...or fresh peaches or strawberries. My brother and I were bribed into turning the crank in exchange for being allowed to lick the paddles.

AUTHOR INDEX